The
5 RULES of
MEGAVALUE
SELLING

The 5 RULES of MEGAVALUE SELLING

How to Communicate Customer Value and Differentiate from Competitors

Mark Holmes

gatekeeper press

Published by Gatekeeper Press
3971 Hoover Rd. Suite 77
Columbus, OH 43123-2839

www.GatekeeperPress.com

ISBN: 9781619846234
eISBN: 9781619846227

Library of Congress Control Number: 2017901015

Printed in the United States of America

To Mom and Dad: A son could not have experienced better parents. I would have loved for you to read this book, but heaven couldn't wait until I finished. You both live on in my heart.

CONTENTS

Contents

PART FOUR: SUCCESS! RESULTS

ACKNOWLEDGEMENTS

WRITING A BOOK is made possible when several people come alongside and help. This book is a testament to that and there are several individuals I'd like to thank.

First and foremost, I'm thankful for my business partner and beautiful wife Jeanna, whose support has been expressed and felt in a million ways during our nearly forty years of marriage. Her belief in me goes way beyond what is deserved, but I definitely benefit from feeling it every day and this encourages me to press onward.

Next, there is a team of people to thank for their helpful suggestions in the early stages of the book. A special thanks goes to two great friends, Bette Price and Larry Labedz. Both of you scoured through the book and held nothing back on how it could be improved.

To David Hammons, I never imagined that coaching you on how to land strategic accounts would one day lead to seeing you author several books, and ultimately to have you provide suggestions and editing for this book – thank you.

To several clients and other reading team members representing various industries, a big thank you goes to Matt Boatright, Ryan Brown, Sandy Higgins, Jeremy Lux, Cary Kapper, Chris Bradshaw and Karen Mitchell. All of you invested

Acknowledgements

personal time in giving me much-needed feedback, and I'm thankful.

Most of all, I am thankful to God for his love through Jesus Christ my Lord, and for enabling me to do what I enjoy.

INTRODUCTION

N O DOUBT THE selling environment today is highly competitive. That's because it's easier today for competitors to mimic one another's products or advantages than it used to be, and it's getting even easier due to technology and the Internet.

Recently, a sales executive client of mine in a billion-dollar energy products and services business expressed his challenge by confessing to me, "If our sales reps differentiated our product value better, they would hit their sales targets." His concern is not uncommon. In fact, studies report that the inability of salespeople to differentiate and sell value messages is the *number one reason* sales targets are not met.

The idea for this book developed over three years. It is both the result of sales managers pointing out to me a need for it, and from observing on various joint sales calls that 95 percent of salespeople struggled with selling value against lower-priced competitors. In addition, roughly 1 out of 10 salespeople had received any coaching or training to develop the capability.

Another challenge to winning sales is noticeable in how customers approach decisions. Contemporary buyers have more information available to them and enjoy more power in the sales cycle. They consider most products and services mere

1

Introduction

commodities and use this belief as an advantage in pushing back on price. This is problematic for salespeople because they must communicate what's different about their product or service from that of their competitors.

The best solution to overcome these challenges is not product, not price or promotion. It is the ability to create high customer perceived value at every phase of the sale. This is the decisive advantage, both because customers want the best value for their money, and because they desire to work with salespeople they can trust.

"Megavalue Selling" is written for anyone at any level who is selling business-to-business products or services. Through the story of a fictional yet realistic company, you will be able to relate to the struggles and triumphs as one sales rep discovers how to apply the five rules of "Megavalue Selling" to close sales.

The ideas and concepts presented in this story are based on realistic events but with fictional organizations. And it doesn't apply only to larger corporations. A small business salesforce, entrepreneurs, financial advisors, insurance agents, business development professionals and consultants have applied these principles as successfully as the salesforce of a large company.

Finally, a brief section at the end of the story summarizes each of the five principles and provides several tips to help you quickly start using the process effectively.

My main purpose for writing this book is to help you communicate and differentiate value in a compelling way. I sincerely hope the ideas in "Megavalue Selling" bring you much future success.

THE FABLE

BACKSTORY

Most selling professionals realized the sales environment had become challenging. Too few, however, had accepted it and adapted successfully to the changes.

Mary Minor was in the camp of the many who did not easily accept or adapt to change. But she did complain about it. She blamed disappointing sales on the economy and complained about losing sales to lower-priced competitors.

The more she complained and the more she blamed lost sales on anyone and anything but herself, the further she moved away from making the necessary changes to turn her situation around.

Unfortunately, it would take an ultimatum from Mary's sales manager to spur her to action. She could not have foreseen what the immediate future had in store for her career at Champs Chemicals.

MARY

SIBLINGS MARK AND Laura Champion co-founded and co-owned Champs Chemicals. The 39-year-old company was located in an industrial hub area of San Antonio, Texas, their birthplace.

The company focused on producing chemicals for applications in a variety of industries, such as automotive, energy, pharmaceutical and technology. Its experienced salesforce sold directly to large end-users, and they sold the company's specialty product line to private label distributors. Champs enjoyed substantial sales and profitability growth during its first 34 years.

Then a severe and prolonged economic downturn occurred.

Sales and profit margins declined. Some competitors reacted by offering lower prices, prompting some of the company's better customers to switch. Morale on the salesforce plummeted as personal sales volume, and bonuses, declined for most of Champs' representatives.

When sales continued to decline, Ethan Ford, the Vice President of Sales, released several sales representatives, including one of their senior account managers, Bob McQueen. He hired new representatives in an attempt to get back lost accounts and land new business.

The Five Rules of Megavalue Selling

One of the company's first new hires was Mary Minor. Most of Bob's accounts were now her responsibility, including most of the customers he had lost to aggressive competitors. Mary's prior sales experience amounted to eight years at two different companies. With the exception of the last couple of years, she had met or exceeded her quotas selling products and services into various industrial markets.

During the course of Ethan's twenty years at Champs, he had rarely experienced a salesperson with Mary's determination and grit. Anyone who was able to hit sales targets in highly competitive industries had to be a little stubborn and persistent. He liked this about Mary and was optimistic that she would be successful in selling the company's product line.

Initially, Mark and Laura Champion were concerned about hiring Mary due to her unfamiliarity with their industry. Sales were about results and whether or not she could sell their products was yet to be seen.

In the end, they sided with Ethan. In the past, he had proven himself an accurate judge of sales potential.

Unsurprisingly, when Mary's performance lagged behind the owners' expectations, they questioned Ethan's decision, especially when he suggested they give her more time. But eventually, they would exert their authority over him and issue an ultimatum.

What no one at Champs recognized about Mary, no one except Ethan that is, was just how successful she could become. Once she discovered what was holding her back from winning more sales and made the necessary changes in her approach, Ethan felt confident Mary would be successful.

Ethan definitely could not have known just how quickly he would be second-guessing his intuition.

Mary

First, Mary would stumble. She would lose another sale again to her foremost competitor. No one would be more upset about this than the owners, and Ethan.

Except, that is, Mary herself.

PART ONE
Underperformance

DISAPPOINTMENT

F RIDAY. FOUR O'CLOCK in the afternoon. Sitting in a tiny meeting room, waiting for thirty minutes on Sally Baker, the CEO of R.S. Baker, a mid-size manufacturer of plastic tubular products.

Mary had called on Sally Baker for three months before being asked to provide a quote on two products. However, a competitor, Henry Barnsdall of QS Supply, was also vying for the order.

Not just any competitor, Henry and QS Supply was Mary's archrival. They were low-ball competitors with a mediocre product line. Somehow though, Henry kept winning sales against Mary.

In the previous six months, Henry had won enough sales to prevent Mary from hitting her last two quarterly targets. Considering QS Supply's inferior products, she struggled to understand how, but still Henry won sale after sale at Mary's expense.

"Hello Mary," Sally Baker said as she charged into the room like someone on a mission. "I'm sorry for running late."

"Not a problem," Mary said smiling. "It's nice seeing you, Sally, and I appreciate your time to talk through my quote."

"Let's see what you have."

Disappointment

Mary took the document from her portfolio and handed it to Sally.

"Okay, let me take a look," Sally said as she quickly flicked through the four pages to the quote located on the last page. "Your price is too high, Mary," she stated.

"Really?" Mary said, surprised. "I know you emphasized how the decision would come down to price, so I even got approval to get you our lowest pricing schedule. I'd really like to get your business and demonstrate to you what we—"

"I understand," Sally interrupted, "but your competitor can give us the same things you're providing plus a little more value and still come under your price."

"What do you mean exactly when you say they gave you a little more value?"

"Well, normally I wouldn't tell you what your competitor did, but you've been professional and a pleasure to work with so I will. QS Supply is providing compliance and documentation help on anything we purchase. This means quite a bit to us because we have a lean staff."

"I didn't know that was important to you. We can provide the same thing and our compliance and documentation folks are—"

Sally nodded but interrupted again. "And QS also extended our finance terms to ninety days versus thirty, which was appealing."

Mary's jaw dropped. "I don't know what to say. Uh, I would have worked on finance terms for you if I had known it was a factor in your decision. But what about quality Sally? We have the most extensive quality control process in the industry and a reputation that's second to none."

Sally raised a hand to stop Mary from continuing. "I know you've promoted your quality to me but look, QS has good quality too. My production supervisor also met with the QS sales rep and he agreed they offer acceptable quality, and he just didn't see any tangible advantage in the value you offered over everything we're getting from QS. So I will be awarding the business to them."

The disappointing news rocked Mary. She was also alarmed to hear about the production supervisor having input to the decision. "Production supervisor? I don't believe I ever met your production supervisor. Does he have input on purchase decisions?"

"Yes," Sally answered. "Frank Roberts has been with us for twenty years. I lean on him for advice. It must have slipped my mind to tell you about him. I'm sorry."

"Oh that's fine," Mary said, hiding her frustration best she could. "I'd like to get his contact information from you before I leave." The pit of disappointment in Mary's stomach grew larger by the minute. She struggled for the right words to say. "When would you suggest I follow-up to see if you have any new needs, changes?"

Sally gave Mary Frank's contact information and said, "Why don't you contact us in October."

"Okay, October, I certainly will," Mary confirmed.

Sally got to her feet and walked around to Mary's side of the table.

They exchanged pleasant goodbyes and Mary left.

FRUSTRATION

Mary breathed a heavy sigh as she walked to her car. *Another lost sale to Henry Barnsdall at QS Supply. I can't believe it!*

As soon as the car door clapped shut she flung the leather sales binder into the backseat, hoping no one saw the outburst. The binder went flying across the seats and onto the floorboard.

"Geez, oh Pete . . . can't I get a break?" she yelled as she turned the ignition and backed out of the visitor's parking stall, beginning the drive back to her office. She'd worked for months to land such a large account and now what did she have to show for it?

Her sales manager, Ethan Ford, would be fuming about her loss of another highly targeted prospect. *How did I screw this up?* she thought. *And how can I be expected to overcome QS's low price?*

"As soon as Ethan finds out I may lose my job!" Mary grumbled aloud.

She agonized over having failed to land this big account, failed to hit her numbers for the past two quarters, and barely made quota before that. She felt like giving up. Quitting.

Only one person believed unconditionally in Mary's potential to be amazing at sales. Fortunately, it was her father, "Pops," as she affectionately referred to him.

Mary eased her company car into a parking space back at the office at five past five. She noticed Ethan's car was gone, along with most of the sales reps' cars. After five on a Friday afternoon, and everyone had gone home for the weekend. *Thank my lucky stars!*

In her office, Mary finished an expense report and entered sales call notes in the company's CRM before collecting her things and heading for Pop's house. Her thoughts stewed with anxiety.

Will Ethan see my notes and call me this weekend, or will he wait until Monday and fire me then? Will I be viewed as a failure?

During the half-hour drive, she fretted about how to tell Pops she was thinking about quitting her sales position. Mary had sought his advice several times, but never concerning her job performance.

It was five miles past her exit before she realized that she was totally absorbed in her concerns.

Mary shook her head with disgust and took the next exit off the highway.

POPS

Pops had enjoyed an extraordinary 25-year career as the number one salesperson at two Fortune 100 companies.

He left to launch an automotive product manufacturing company, personally built sales to over $20 million, and sold the company for a tidy profit. With the money he earned, he eventually bought four struggling businesses, including an AM radio station and a business services company. He turned sales around at those companies, too.

Others noticed his insights on sales and he was asked to speak at conferences and do training seminars. Pops felt a great sense of satisfaction helping others and he willingly shared his insights with anyone.

When Pop's wife of 33 years died from an aggressive form of liver cancer, he was decimated. He immediately sold two of his businesses to spend more time with Mary and her two brothers, volunteer at his church, and help out with his favorite charities.

Mary inched along towards Pop's driveway feeling anxious. One of the things he had always emphasized was not quitting easily. Now she worried about his reaction to her situation. *How will he respond? Will Pops be disappointed in me?*

His opinion still greatly mattered to her. Even though they

hadn't seen eye to eye on everything, Pops was still her biggest encourager. She knew he would support whatever she decided to do with her career.

She gave a soft knock, then opened the door to her family home.

EXCUSES

MARY WALKED IN and plopped onto the couch, and said, "This is a lousy day!"

Mary was a mirror image of her late mother. Beautiful blonde hair, model-like frame, and gorgeous looks that attracted a steady stream of boys to their home when she was a teen, much to Pop's displeasure.

Pops walked towards the couch, and said, "What's wrong?"

Mary sighed, biting her lip before admitting, "I failed to hit my numbers again!" She looked at the awards and framed pictures hanging above the mantle of Pops shaking hands with business leaders. Deliberately, she avoided his gaze. "I'm failing and I'm thinking about quitting before they fire me."

He sat in the wooden rocker next to his daughter. He wasn't sure what to say, or do. "What's keeping you from making your sales numbers?"

"That's easy!" Mary said with a cynical huff. "The economy isn't helping me out, a lot of prospective customers are already happy with their present supplier, and the products I sell are getting hammered by competitors offering low-ball pricing. I could hit my numbers easily if it weren't for all that."

Pops nodded. "Sounds like you have the *if only* disease."

Mary furrowed her brows. "What does that mean?"

"*If only* I had this product to sell, or *if only* I had that price to work with, or *if only* that was different or this was better, then I could sell."

Mary rolled her eyes, knowing he was right but still wanting to deny it. "I'm not the only one struggling. It's hard to make sales right now with this economy, competitors' pricing, uncertainty over the future . . ."

"Yeah, it is tough to make sales today! But it always is, and you're making it harder than it needs to be," Pops countered. He waited for her to respond but she didn't.

"Would you agree that there are things we can control as a salesperson, and things we can't control?" Pops pressed on.

"Yes," Mary answered.

"So then, if we focus our thoughts on what we *can't* control instead of what we *can* control, what's the impact on sales?"

"Hurts my sales."

"Precisely," said Pops. "Is it possible you are focusing on things you can't control—like the economy, competitors and the customers' indifference? And aren't you overlooking the things you can control?"

"Like what?"

"Like your attitude, actions, and your approach to selling. Aren't those within your control?"

Mary nodded. "I agree. I think my attitude is generally pretty good," she said raising her eyebrows, "but where I'd like some fresh insight and possible help is with my sales approach."

REALITY CHECK

"So why do you think you lost the sale today?" Pops asked Mary.

"My price was too high," she answered boldly.

"How can you be so sure it was price?"

"Because I shot them our very lowest price and the competitor undercut me," Mary explained, crossing her arms tight across her chest.

Pops stroked his chin, deep in thought for several seconds. "That doesn't sound like a price issue to me."

"Why not?"

"For starters, did your customer actually tell you that your price caused you to lose the sale?

"Not exactly. She gave me some mumbo jumbo about receiving more overall value from my competitor."

"So maybe it wasn't about the lowest price – maybe it was value."

Mary shook her head. "No, my customer told me early on that the decision would be based on the lowest price."

"And you believed them?"

"Of course, I didn't have a choice."

"Oh yes you did," Pops said. "Instead of unwittingly making

the discussion about price, you should have made the discussion about value."

"I have to take my customer at their word when they say price is all that matters," Mary insisted.

Pops said adamantly, "Not if you want to win more sales."

"Afraid I just don't see it," Mary said shaking her head. "How can you be so sure?"

"Good question," Pops said. "First of all, studies show that only about five percent of purchase decisions are based on price alone. This means ninety-five percent of your customers include additional factors in their decision-making process. Secondly, ask yourself something: Do you think customers would actually turn a blind eye to crucial factors like quality, performance, reliability, on-time delivery, service or trust when it comes to which supplier to use? Ignore it all and go only with lowest price?"

After considering Pop's point, Mary said, "Then why do customers say it's all about price if it's really not?"

"Because it's effective," Pops responded. "It's a negotiation tactic and it gets salespeople to low-bid their price. Let's approach this with an analogy for a moment.

"Let's say you were looking at three 1 Carat diamonds in a jewelry store and all the diamonds appeared very similar. However, the price points on the rings varied considerably. Would you just pick the cheapest diamond because they all looked similar to you? Or, would you want to know the qualities of each diamond before you made your decision?"

"Obviously I'd want to know about their quality, cut, color, clarity, the bling factor . . ."

Pops laughed. "God help the man you marry someday!"

Mary smiled briefly at the thought but quickly pressed

on. "Seriously, so you're saying my customers have the same concerns. They want value. Is that right?"

"That's pretty close." Pops stood and walked to the antique secretary desk. He located a promotional flyer and handed it to her.

"What's this?" Mary asked pausing to examine the piece.

"A promotion I got from the local zoo!" Pops said laughing. Mary glanced at the headline and laughed. "Oh my gosh!

BEST ZOO POO ON THE PLANET. Improves fertility. Enhances root penetration. Increases aeration. No other poo compares! Gives you better water and nutrient retention. Matches the needs of plants. Provides your garden with the trace minerals that offer a healthier diet for you and your family. Get Your Zoo Poopy Doo Today!

"Not to be crass," Pops said, smiling, "but if you can differentiate crap you can differentiate anything!"

Mary laughed at Pop's joke, but at the same time she recognized his point. "Differentiating my products' value when competitors have very similar options is difficult. But I guess it's my job—"

"Yes, definitely!" Pops said with a confirming nod.

"So, I've got a question for you," Mary said as she set the flyer aside.

"I'll do my best to answer it."

"How exactly did you achieve so much success selling in different industries? What did you do?"

Pops chuckled. "Rather than tell you what I did, let me first show you what guided me on the road to more success than I ever imagined possible. I'll be right back."

Pops stood and walked down the hallway.

THE REMINDERS

POPS RETURNED HOLDING a scuffed-up, brown leather journal. He beamed with pride and gave it to Mary.

"Here," Pops announced, "I want you to have this."

"What is it?" Mary asked.

"I call it *The Book of Reminders*. Over the years, I recorded the insights that helped me sell value and win so many sales. But don't get the wrong impression," Pops said with a smile, "I learned from making lots of mistakes, and I had some great mentors, too."

"Very, very interesting . . ." Mary thumbed through the pages. "This is kind of like a book of motivation tips and secrets?"

"No, not that kind of book. Motivation is essential, but if you want to win more sales in today's business environment you need knowledge, not just inspiration. The *Book of Reminders* is a practical book with tips on how to sell value successfully."

"Well, you certainly profited from them," Mary noted.

"Yes, I've been blessed more than I deserve," said Pops. "But one of my greatest joys comes from sharing and watching others increase their success from using the Reminders—"

"My brothers!" exclaimed Mary. "You've already shared this with Jeb and Chip, haven't you?"

Pops hesitated and then admitted, "Yes, I did."

The Reminders

"Why haven't you shared it with me?"

"Well," Pops said, "when your brothers experienced a similar sales challenge they came to me and asked for help, just like you are doing now."

Mary sighed. She regretted not asking for his help earlier in her career. "You know, it's hard for me to ask for help because I want to figure things out on my own. Guess I can be a little stubborn."

"Who you?" Pops said as he turned and flicked a piece of lint from his jeans. "Nah, I'd never describe you as a *little* stubborn." He looked at Mary, chuckled, and gave her a big wink.

That made Mary smile. Once more she focused her attention on *The Book of Reminders*. She slowly turned the pages. "So basically, the Reminders will help . . ." Mary said, continuing to scan its contents. "Will it help me sell value more convincingly?"

Pops smiled and nodded.

"Where should I start?"

"Let's start with selling to customers who resist your price," Pops said gesturing for the book.

Mary handed him the Reminders and said, "I can't wait."

24

FOCUS ON VALUE

Pops turned to the page and asked Mary to read the Reminder.

All customers want a lower price, but none want lower value. When your customer focuses on price, focus on value.

"What do you think about this Reminder?" asked Pops.

"Great point," said Mary. "Like you said, ninety-five percent of the time value and not just price influences a customer's decision. But it still doesn't answer my real dilemma."

Pops smiled. "What's your dilemma?"

"Let's start with how I can get a customer to see that my value is superior to the competition. If that's okay?"

"Good idea." He walked over to the large living room windows and said, "You know, I've seen a lot of 'pitchy' salespeople in the various industries I've worked in over the years—and I have a recent example that could shed some light on your challenge."

"Sounds good."

"Recently, a large tax and accounting services firm wanted me to help them increase business. So I did ride-along sales calls with their business development people. Early in the sales conversation, the firm's salespeople typically presented an avalanche of purchase reasons to the customer. They talked about how long their firm had been in business, about their great services, they bragged about the firm's customer list, and so on. You get the picture I'm sure. How do you think the prospects responded to the pitch?"

"Uh, probably indifferent, non-committal or uh, even turned off."

"You nailed it! The real question is, why?" Pops asked.

"Because it sounded like a sales pitch," Mary said.

"Good, okay. And why do sales pitches fall short of buyers' interests or expectations?"

"Maybe because they've heard the same kinds of pitches from other firms or suppliers," Mary said as her mind continued searching for reasons. "I'd also say that customers find it difficult to see the potential value of a product or service to their business when it's communicated as a generic pitch."

"Exactly," said Pops. "The pitch may sound impressive but it fails to approach the purchase from the buyer's concerns."

He continued, "It's like purchasing anything. If you don't have the extra time or expertise to quantify the value of one supplier versus another, you welcome working with a salesperson who will be a trusted resource and help you make an informed decision."

An example came to Mary's mind, and she said, "Sort of like the pool salesman you purchased from several years ago?"

"Yes! I probably told you the story about him. How he first qualified us and gained an understanding of our desires and needs. He asked questions that caused us to consider features and possible problems we hadn't included in our decision. He also introduced new features that would give us more long-term value . . ."

BANG!

26

The Five Rules of Megavalue Selling

The loud noise caused Pop's five-year-old cat, Chumley, to bolt from the dining room chair where he had been curled up asleep and jump onto Mary's lap. "Chumley!" Mary said, surprised. "Everything's okay, ol' boy."

"A truck backfired," Pops said as he snickered at Chumley. Mary smiled at Chumley as she scratched the top of his head and he purred loudly. She looked at Pops and said, "So were you always amazing at sales?"

"Ha! In the beginning, I was mediocre at best."

"You're kidding?"

Pops shook his head, and said, "Nope. I wasn't able to sell my product's value as well as I needed to. In fact, it wasn't until I hit my Big Awareness Moment that my success accelerated."

"Your big . . . awareness . . . moment? What happened?"

"Well, one day my sales manager decided to go on ride-along sales calls. He didn't say it, but I'm sure he wanted to see why my sales were lagging. After the first few sales calls, he basically let me have it."

"What did he say?"

"He wanted to know where I had learned to sell. I told him I learned from some books I'd read."

"And his response?" Mary asked.

Pops grimaced. "He told me I needed to take an honest look at myself in the mirror if I wanted to be better at selling."

"Yeah . . . and?"

"And what I saw in my technique was a salesman who loved bragging about his products, his company, and cutting prices in order to land the sale. How many customers are going to buy from a salesperson if they can't convince them of their value?"

"Right," Mary said. "Especially if your emphasis is on matching prices with cheaper competitors."

"It's funny you say that," Pops said. He grabbed *The Book of*

Reminders and slowly ticked through the pages until he found what he wanted. "Here it is!" Pops said as he handed the book to Mary and pointed to the Reminder.

Your price matters LEAST when you make your value matter MOST. Present a compelling value message.

Mary started to ask a question but the vibration of her cell phone stopped her cold. She feared it might be her boss, Ethan Ford, Vice President of Sales.

"Gotta take this, Pops, it's my boss," Mary said as her heart raced anxiously.

ANXIETY

"Hello, Ethan," Mary answered, dreading the inevitable. "I'm sorry I lost the R.S. Baker sale but—" she continued, but Ethan interrupted her. She bit her lip and listened.

Pops paid close attention as she answered, "Yes, we got beat on price but she also said that they didn't see enough difference in our products."

Mary shrank into the couch as Ethan asked questions in quick succession like a defense attorney cross-examining a witness.

"I do understand, it's just—" Mary's face flushed red with irritation as Ethan interrupted her again.

"Who won the sale? QS Supply did," Mary answered.

Ethan immediately wanted to know why she'd lost another customer to QS Supply. She told him, "Because they felt QS offered better overall value at a lower price."

Mary looked at the area rug covering the floor under her feet. She rested the phone on her ear and took a deep breath.

"Okay, yes," Mary said, "I'll see you first thing Monday morning." When the conversation ended, Mary looked out the window, trying to regain her composure.

Anxiety

Pops seemed especially concerned. "What did Ethan say, Mary?"

"I don't want to talk about it," Mary answered, still staring out the window.

Almost a full minute passed before Mary spoke. "So this was your secret to being so successful in sales?" she asked looking at *The Book of Reminders* clasped between her hands.

"It was indeed," said Pops with a gleam in his eye. "Do you want to dig into this again tomorrow?"

Mary shook her head. "No, I want to think about what I've learned today, and I want to read more of the Reminders over the weekend. Monday's an important day . . ."

Pops gave Mary a warm smile and walked her to the door. "Let me know what happens on Monday, please."

Mary smiled and thanked Pops again. She left his house worried about Monday. *Will I get fired? Is Ethan being pressured by the owners to fire me?*

Later that evening Mary sunk herself into her overstuffed couch with *The Book of Reminders* and a box of Milk Duds, her favorite comfort food. She began reading. Monday would come too soon.

TENSION

ETHAN EASED HIS SUV into its usual parking space and grabbed his briefcase. Monday mornings always began in a meeting with Laura and Mark Champion at 7:00 a.m.

The elevator *dinged*. He stepped out and headed for his office to gather some reports he'd prepared for the meeting. Then Ethan made his way to the boardroom, where he knew Mark and Laura were waiting.

He decided to start with the tough topic first. "Mary blew the R.S. Baker account?" Laura repeated. "I hope you're planning to cut her loose."

"She's right, Ethan, Mary's got to go," Mark Champion insisted.

"Selecting and training her replacement will take precious time we don't have," Ethan said, raising his voice slightly. "Mary knows the territory, her customers like her, her product knowledge is good and . . ." He straightened his sport jacket to control his anxiety. "I want to keep her for two more months to see what she can do."

"For what reason?" Mark asked, glaring across the table at Ethan.

"I want to give her two months to see if she can rise to the challenge. Then—"

"That doesn't make any sense!" Mark interrupted. "Her numbers have been disappointing for six months now."

"But remember," Ethan said, ignoring Mark's tone, "Mary has won back a couple of large accounts we never thought we'd see again."

Mark sat there with a scowl, arms folded, looking at his sister. Laura, the younger and calmer of the two said, "Ethan, I think you ought to go ahead and retain Mary if that's what you want. It's your call. But she must turn it around in sixty days. Period."

After a few moments of awkward silence, Mark Champion stated, "It's your call, like Laura said. You are responsible for the results. Mary has sixty days to start hitting her numbers. That's it."

Ethan quickly thanked Mark and Laura and returned to his office.

Mary faced a giant-sized challenge and Ethan didn't waste a second calling her to his office.

LAST CHANCE

E THAN LOOKED THE part of a successful executive: dressed
in charcoal grey slacks with a white, oxford shirt and an
expensive black blazer that accentuated his striking gray hair.
When Mary arrived at his office, he had just poured a cup of
coffee.

"Hello Mary, have a seat," he said matter-of-factly. "I'll get
right to the point. I met with Mark and Laura this morning and
they are very disappointed that you lost the R.S. Baker account.
Also, the fact that your numbers are suffering has them very
upset.

"Looking back, I regret not spending more time coaching
and doing joint calls with you," Ethan said wringing his hands.
"I don't know, maybe it would have helped. Here's the bottom
line, and I'm sorry it comes down to this, but you have sixty
days to turn things around. That is, if you want to stick it out?"

Mary had prepared herself for this outcome, but not for the
sting she suddenly felt to her self-esteem. She gathered herself
with a quick, silent breath. "You bet I do," she said with an
enthusiastic nod.

Ethan smiled and said, "Excellent, I'm glad you aren't quitting
on me."

"I do have one question, though," Mary said.

"Okay."

"What do I need to do to prove myself?"

"Glad you asked," Ethan said. "There are a couple of things, beginning with improving your sales approach—not your sales activity because that's fine. Specifically, you must find a way to close more sales without always cutting the price. And one other thing, you've got to differentiate our product line. You're losing sales to inferior competitors . . ."

"Okay, I'll do my best," Mary said and offered another eager nod.

"Your best won't cut it," Ethan replied. "You've got to *up* your game and win some sales, soon."

Mary nodded, acknowledging what he was saying. "You mentioned there were a couple of things I must do to prove myself," Mary said. "What's the second?"

"Yes, here it is." Ethan reached across his desk and thumbed through a stack of customer file folders. He selected three.

PROVE YOURSELF

Ethan handed Mary the three files and said, "You want to know how you can prove yourself to Mark and Laura, and to me? Well here you go. Don't lose any of your current customer business and land these three large accounts."

"All three in sixty days?" Mary asked.

"Ideally, yes, but realistically, you must win at least one. Please listen while I give you some background on Sphere Resources, AB ProPlastics, and Twig Enterprises.

"Let's start with AB ProPlastics because they used to be a loyal customer. Bob, your predecessor, lost their business and blamed it on a competitor offering the same products at lower prices. He made several attempts to get them back but failed.

"Next, there's Sphere Resources. They have big potential and they're a huge player in their niche. It was a lead Bob failed to convert because he said they were happy with their present supplier. If you win either of these two accounts it would go a long way to impressing Laura and Mark—get my drift?"

Mary smiled. "Got it. Maybe even save my job?"

"Maybe."

"Why haven't these three accounts been assigned to me before now?" Mary inquired.

"Honestly, because I wasn't confident you would be successful and they have huge potential," Ethan answered. "Now, I've saved the best for last, sort of. Five years ago, Twig Enterprises was one of our company's largest accounts. And now, they do zero sales with us. The main decision-maker is Duncan Quinn and he is difficult to deal with. He hasn't let anyone from Champs have an appointment in six months; not me and not Mark Champion. Mark tried three times but got rejected each time. He probably won't take or return any of your calls or emails. If you did win Twig back, it would be the sales miracle of the year!"

"What are the odds I can land Twig?"

"I just said it would be a miracle," Ethan said. Then he added, smiling, "let's just say I'll be shocked if you land a meeting, let alone land their business—but you have to try because Mark wants Twig back badly."

"So which account has the highest priority?" Mary asked, thumbing through the files.

"It's your decision, not mine. You need to sell all three, so contact all three in one week or spread them out. Doesn't matter to me."

"What I meant to ask was, who should I start with?"

"I just told you, that's not my decision," Ethan answered. "You've tried two times to get me to make a simple decision for you, and honestly, it's a little irritating. I'm counting on you to take ownership of these accounts. My neck is on the line with Mark and Laura, too. Now don't let me down."

Mary nodded. She stared at the three customer files.

Ethan drummed his fingers on his armrest.

His silence made her uneasy.

Mary drew in a bottomless breath, and said as she exhaled, "I won't disappoint you. I'll find a way to close these accounts."

Mary stood with confidence, thanked Ethan and then she left.

On the way back to her desk, Mary's head was spinning as she tried to figure everything out. *I need to review the CRM and customer files on each of these accounts. I need to set priorities. I need a game plan. And I need to speak with Pops.*

That afternoon, she called Pops and told him what Ethan had said. "I'd like to come over tonight. I have a few questions," she told him.

"Sure thing, I'll have a pot of coffee on!" Pops said.

PART TWO
ROADMAP TO RESULTS

ROADMAP

Pops had just checked on the coffee when he heard Mary's car door close. He met her at the front door with a cup and a big smile. "Dark roast with a small shot of cream?"

"Awesome, thanks!" Mary said, taking the cup as she walked inside.

She sat and placed *The Book of Reminders* on her lap. "I'm not sure where to start, Pops, but I'll give you a quick overview."

Mary summarized the three assigned accounts, revisiting Ethan's comments and filling Pops in on the ultimatum by the Champion siblings. Her pinched face showed the strain she felt from her situation. Pops nodded with concern at each detail of Mary's predicament.

Chumley, roused by their conversation, strutted into the living room. He angled over to Mary and began purring and rubbing his thick black fur all over her tan slacks, twisting and turning around her legs.

Mary placed Chumley on a nearby blanket and looked at Pops. "I read the entire *Book of Reminders* in a few hours. It's excellent and don't get me wrong, but—"

"But what?"

"I've been thinking," Mary said with hesitation, "if the

Reminders were in a simple, organized process, maybe a few steps—"

"Got you covered!" Pops said smiling. "Over the years, I came to the conclusion that the value of every business product or service can be differentiated successfully if five rules are followed. I put those rules into a sales approach I refer to as, *Megavalue Selling.*"

Mary turned her head, and said, "Megavalue Selling? Five rules? What are they and what do they involve?"

Pops smiled at Mary's interest. "Megavalue Selling involves two things," he said. "First, it involves communicating convincingly to the customer what differentiates your product's value from others."

"You have examples?"

"I can give you plenty. It could be something that your product, service or your company does faster, better, safer or in a manner less costly. Or, you might provide higher quality, less risk, or greater reliability and performance. Any attribute your customer views as a benefit to them, can be used to differentiate your value."

Mary listened carefully and made a few quick notes.

Pops continued. "Megavalue Selling also involves, and this is an important point—" he said pausing, "it involves outselling your competitor when you don't have clear product superiority—and that means selling your value through each stage of the customer's decision-making process."

"Hold on, I want to clarify this," said Mary. "You're saying that I should sell the superiority of my product, if it is clearly superior, but still outsell my competitor if I don't have product superiority?"

Pops nodded insistently.

The Five Rules of Megavalue Selling

"Okay," Mary said. "But how am I supposed to outsell my competition when I don't have superiority?"

"The five rules of Megavalue Selling give you a roadmap to follow, whether you have superiority or not."

Pops grabbed a notebook, tore off a sheet of paper and drew a triangle. He divided the triangle into five sections by drawing four lines across. "It's not how I planned it, but the five rules actually spell *value*.

"I'd like you to understand the concept because it's made all the difference to my success. If you find it's beneficial, I'd love to see you share the knowledge of Megavalue Selling with others."

Mary nodded slowly, taking it all in.

"Now then, each time we meet we will fill in the triangle and discuss each of the five rules," he continued. "You will see that they're simple and very practical. But don't be misled, the real challenge is to put them to use.

"So let's start with the first rule: **V**," Pops said.

V - VERIFY VALUE DRIVERS

Pops looked at the triangle and labeled the top section *V- Verify Value Drivers.*

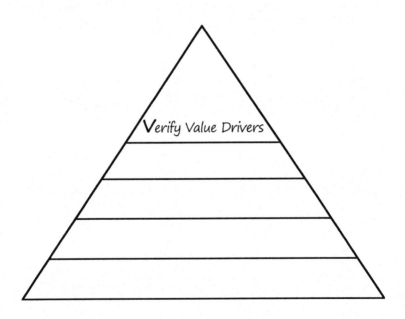

"Verify Value Drivers is the one behavior that influences all others," he explained. "If you don't do a sufficient job at verifying your customer's value drivers, your value message suffers. Let me describe it this way.

"Attempting to sell your value without knowing your customer's value drivers is like trying to hit a target from a hundred yards away with a blindfold on. You can guess where the bulls-eye is, and you might get lucky and hit it. But it's doubtful."

"I get it," Mary said. "But what *are* value drivers exactly, and do you have any examples I can identify with?"

"Good questions. Let's begin with defining value drivers. Basically, value drivers are the resulting benefits, or value, the customer expects from your products or services," Pops said. "You see, customers don't just buy a product—they buy what a product provides to them initially and what it delivers longer-term.

"For example, suppose you are trying to sell insurance. People don't buy an insurance policy; they buy the value of how it reduces their risk, gives them peace of mind, better coverage or a lower cost. Or if you sell accounting or financial services, for example, customers aren't buying your time, they are buying the desired outcomes you can produce such as tax advice, and a great return on their investments."

Mary concentrated on Pop's explanation, and said, "I'm beginning to get the picture of value drivers now."

"Good," Pops said. "So do you see how value drivers impact every type of sales conversation? Whether it's selling services, software, storage tanks or manufactured goods—it doesn't matter because customers buy in order to get specific benefits or results. And those desired benefits or results are their value drivers."

Mary nodded. "You're saying I must sell to the customer's value drivers because that's driving their purchase. Ultimately, value drivers influence which company the customer chooses to purchase from. Correct?"

"Exactly! Now, you also asked for some examples earlier, so let me suggest some very common value drivers."

With her pen and notebook ready for action Mary said, "Go for it."

"Most business customers desire products or services that help them save money, make money, save time, avoid or solve a problem. Those kinds of desired outcomes are common. But, there are other value drivers that are more specific to your customer's situation.

"For example, your customer may also want a product that lowers risk, improves safety, increases productivity, will be delivered on-time, or improves quality and performance. Or, they may desire solutions to increase product inventory turns, prevent future problems, avoid headaches, improve technology or give them guaranteed results. The list is virtually endless.

"Most important," Pops added, "is to be one hundred percent certain you know each customer's value drivers."

"How can I be one hundred percent certain?"

Pops reached for a folder and withdrew a single sheet of paper which he handed to Mary.

"What's this?"

"Basic questions you can ask to identify your customer's value drivers," Pops answered. "Good questions do three things: they engage your customer in useful conversation, they help create trust earlier and faster, and questions help you determine whether or not your product is a good fit for them.

"If the customer isn't going to be a good fit for your company, or you determine that their preference for another supplier is too strong for you to overcome, it's a good time to bow out.

The Five Rules of Megavalue Selling

"Go back to the value drivers I listed off earlier, please. Can you identify the most common value drivers for your customers?"

Mary looked over the list. She nodded immediately.

"Good. Okay, now look it over and identify any value drivers that customers tend to undervalue or overlook entirely in their purchase decision, but shouldn't. Do you see any?"

"Oh yeah!" Mary said. "Like quality and on-time delivery. Those sometimes are viewed as less important than price concerns."

"But are they less important?"

"Absolutely not!" Mary answered.

"Good, very good," Pops said. "So those basic questions in your hand will help you uncover your customer's existing value drivers as well as any drivers not factored into their decision, but that should be."

Mary eagerly glanced over the questions.

- What factors or criteria will drive your decision?

- What are the most significant challenges you face?

- What results do you want us to deliver?

- What problem do you want solved (or avoided)?

- What needs are you most concerned about on this project?

- How quickly do you want to get moving on a solution?

- What kind of priority does this have for you?

- If this does not get solved satisfactorily, what is the impact?

"There are a lot of good questions here," Mary said after taking her time reviewing. She fidgeted with her pen as she marked several questions she liked. "I'd like to ask better questions, like these."

"You can, and you will with practice," Pop said as he reached for the sheet of questions in her hand. "Start by taking these questions and modifying them for your customers. This is easier to do if you've done your homework. For example, you want to understand your customer's industry, their challenges, their customers, competitors, the company's decision influencers and the buying process, budget and timeline."

Pops liked that Mary was making notes, and said, "You may already be doing this, and if you are, you realize that a solid understanding helps you engage the customer in conversation."

Pops and Mary spent several minutes going over examples of questions and discussing how to modify them for her sales opportunities.

"I see how asking the right questions allows me to pinpoint each customer's particular issues and value drivers," Mary said as she rubbed Chumley. "But I've got a bigger problem."

"All right, what is it?"

"I'm having trouble differentiating my product from a competitor with a similar product line, similar pricing and good service. I've tried explaining it several different ways but I just . . ."

"Don't feel like you're the only one," Pops said. "Most salespeople struggle with differentiating their product from competitors—and it's clearly because there's so much parity among companies."

Pops shifted his lean frame around in the chair, and said, "In fact, I was in the middle of a sales presentation once when the customer interrupted me, and said, 'I can get the identical product from your competitor a lot cheaper!' When I responded with more reasons from my company's playbook, something I'd been taught to do, he said to me, 'Theirs does the very same thing.' So I answered with even more reasons and before I could get very far he cut me off and said, 'Their product has the same features, but lots cheaper.'"

"What happened then?" Mary really wanted to know.

"You can probably guess what happened," said Pops. "He ended the meeting abruptly and I left defeated and discouraged."

"Did you learn from your mistake?"

Pops chuckled and said, "You bet I did! When I finally figured out what I was doing wrong, I stopped putting prospects through an information landslide. Instead, I began asking questions to uncover their value drivers."

"Otherwise you couldn't sell to your customers' drivers."

"Precisely," said Pops. "Once I realized the bulls-eye my value message must hit, I could tailor it to my customers' specific interest and increase their perceived value of my product. And, as you can probably guess, my sales took off then."

Mary sat back in her seat for a moment. "It can't be this easy."

"It's not easy!" Pops said. "But it's also not overly-complex to differentiate between products or services, if you know how."

"This makes a lot more sense to me now," Mary said. "I think I'm ready for the next rule. Will you tell me what the **A** stands for?"

Pops smiled and reached for his pen.

A-ADAPT YOUR VALUE MESSAGE

M ARY WATCHED POPS as he filled in the next line of the triangle.

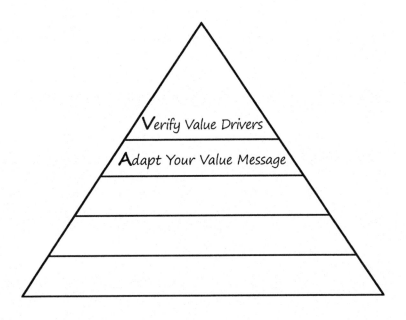

"So the **A** stands for Adapt Your Value Message?" Mary asked.

"Yes, and when you use this rule consistently you should get better customer responsiveness to your message, and better sales."

"You have my undivided attention!" Mary said with a grin.

Pops got a chuckle out of Mary's comment. "Good! Now then, Adapt Your Value Message is not difficult to do. It involves taking what you learn when you Verify Value Drivers and adapting your value message to link with those drivers."

"Do you have a cheat sheet I can use?" Mary said half-jokingly.

"I'll do one better. There are just a couple of practical steps to this. First, you want to sell to your customer's existing value drivers. If you can't convince them your product satisfies their current requirements, it's unlikely you'll win the sale. Second, you want to introduce additional value drivers that are *not* influencing your customer's decision at the moment, but really should. Earlier, I termed these value drivers 'overlooked' or 'undervalued' drivers."

"Yeah, I remember!" Mary remarked with enthusiasm. "You asked me to identify value drivers that I think my buyers overlook or undervalue and I mentioned a couple. But now, several others come to mind."

"Like what?"

"Actually, several aspects regarding safety come to mind. Also, new product compliance requirements, inventory management and even opportunities to improve profit margins are often ignored or undervalued by prospects that are singularly focused on price."

"Great point!" Pops complimented.

"Thanks, but I'll admit, this is not something I've been doing."

"Mary, everyone has a blind spot, or two. This is your blind spot and it was also one of mine—that is until I became aware of it and made the necessary changes."

"How did you become aware of it?"

"Thankfully, a competitor pointed it out!" Pops said.

Mary's eyes flashed with interest. She placed her pen to one side, and said, "What happened?"

"Well, one morning I saw this competitor of mine in the diner I frequented," Pops began. "Now, he was a veteran salesman and had been kicking my butt, winning sales and taking accounts away from me right and left. He was eating alone so I sat at his booth and introduced myself.

"He said, *'I know who you are. What can I do for you?'*

"*You consistently beat me in this territory. What do you do, come in with low-dollar pricing?*" I asked him.

"He looked me in the eyes and said calmly, *'Nope. My pricing is usually a little higher. Your problem is you haven't accepted the truth about our customers when it comes to winning sales.'*

"*What truth?*" I wanted to know.

'Look, he said, *I probably shouldn't be telling you this but I'm retiring next week so I'll tell you honestly. You haven't recognized that most sales aren't lost due to higher perceived price but to lower perceived value. You aren't getting significantly out-priced by me; you're getting significantly outsold.'*

"*Outsold?* I repeated. *What do you mean significantly outsold?*"

'I mean,' he said, *'that you have a blind spot.'*

"His remark surprised me. "*You think I have a blind spot?*"

'Yes I do,' he answered. *'The primary reason customers buy from me and not you is that they believe I offer better value than you do. Initially, I don't try to convince a prospect to buy. Instead I gain an in-depth understanding of what they want to achieve, or the problem they want to solve. Then I adjust my sales message to fit their desires and introduce any information or product advantages they ought to consider but haven't. Only then do I*

switch gears and focus on the impact my product will have on their situation.

'Now,' he said, glaring at me, '*you're the only one benefitting from this conversation and you are wasting my time. Good day.*'

"I remember walking out stunned. My head was spinning with excitement, confusion, and all sorts of emotions. His comments had infuriated me, but the truth does cut deeply."

Not knowing what else to say, Mary asked, "what did you do?"

"I thought about it for a few days and realized I could either learn from his feedback, or deny it. My method was producing mediocre results because I neglected adapting my value message to fit each of my customer's situations. I needed to skill up, basically."

"Hmmm," Mary said. She thought through her own situation. "That's basically where I am right now. I could have a lot more success if I tailored my value message to the customer's specific situation and drivers."

Pops nodded and smiled.

"Hey, I recall reading a Reminder . . ." Mary said as she turned the pages of *The Book of Reminders*, "where is it . . . oh, here it is."

Mary showed it to Pops.

Your WORDS make buyers think. CONVICTION makes them feel. But your VALUE linked to their value drivers makes them buy.

"This is the point exactly," Pops said. "Until my encounter with the competitor, I couldn't understand why prospects were continually raising objections like, 'You're too expensive,' 'We're happy with our current provider,' and 'Your product is just like everyone else's.'

"Once I recognized my shortcomings, I immediately began verifying value drivers and adapting my value message to the customer's drivers on every sales call," Pops said.

"Did it improve your results?"

"Absolutely!" Pops replied. "It gave me an effective way to differentiate my product from others. Customers quickly showed increased interest. I started winning more sales and busted some all-time sales records. What's really amazing was when I left that business to sell for a professional services company, Megavalue Selling paid off big time there too."

Mary stared right past Pops for several seconds, then said, "If selling value works so well, why don't more salespeople do it?"

"I think they would if they knew how. The reason isn't that salespeople don't want to sell value. It's because they don't know how, especially against competitors with similar offers."

He pointed to the triangle on the sheet of paper he'd been using and said, "In my experience most reps don't take an Adapt Your Value Message approach to selling value. They use a 'one size fits all' approach instead. Or, we might relate it to baking a dozen cookies with a cookie cutter—all the cookies turn out looking and tasting the same."

"This makes me think," Mary said.

"Great," said Pops. "If you examined your current approach to selling value, would you say it's a 'one size fits all' or not?"

"Unfortunately, I've been in a rut of giving a 'one size fits all' message, rather than tailoring my message to fit their individual businesses."

"And how's that worked out for you?"

"You already know the answer."

Pops nodded.

"There is one problem I see with trying to sell a value message that is tailored to the customer's situation," Mary said.

"What do you mean?

"Well, a lot of customers are closed-minded and not truly open to having their opinions challenged." Mary said this with conviction but she could tell by Pop's facial expression that he didn't agree.

"Really?" Pops said. "Isn't that shortsighted?"

"No. Why is that shortsighted?"

"Suppose your customer has reached an incorrect conclusion or assumption about your product. The customer isn't always right, so isn't it risky to avoid confronting those false beliefs or opinions?"

"Maybe," Mary said. "But shouldn't I feel like the customer is open to being challenged, first? Um, I don't want to look like I'm being pushy."

"That's an excuse," Pops said. "When you challenge customers in a professional manner they don't view it as being pushy. In fact, most appreciate it. You see, turning your buyer's pushback or inaccurate belief into a learning point gives them value—and you become a trusted advisor in their eyes. That's a win-win!"

"I just don't know if I can sell that way."

"Then you have two choices. Let your customer form his or her own impression of your product's value and do nothing to change it. Or, second, you can address any information gaps, assumptions, or preconceived ideas about your product through professional, tactful conversation.

"Now, if you are unwilling to do this," Pops said, "and would rather let your customer believe whatever they want, then you're selling on the hope customers will fully appreciate and understand your value, to the point they will purchase it over all other choices—even lower-priced suppliers with comparable offers."

Mary sat back in her chair and stared at the ceiling. "Umm, that leaves a lot to pure chance."

"Sure does," Pops agreed. "Nowadays, customers want their sales rep to be a resource, to have expertise and insights to help them make informed decisions and get the best value for their money.

"How do you think a salesperson is viewed by a customer if they fail to bring fresh insights, ask thought-provoking, challenging questions, and bring little value to the conversation?"

"That's a very good question," Mary said. "It makes me wonder how customers actually view me?"

"And how do you think they view you? Honestly."

"Customers probably view me as a sales rep who sells virtually the same products they can get from ten other suppliers."

Pops nodded. "But now you know what to do in order to stand out among your competitors and get better results."

"Yes, and I'm pumped about putting this knowledge to work with my new opportunities. Okay, I'm ready for the **L** rule!" Mary said.

"Excellent," said Pops. "But we're not going to talk about that right now. There's something else I want to discuss first."

E – EMPHASIZE EVIDENCE

POPS GRASPED THE piece of paper and said, "It's time for a change in direction. We're going to move down to the last rule, the E. However, we'll continue referring to the need for verifying and adapting value. So unless you have a question . . ."

Mary liked Pop's pace. He stopped to explain things and gave her examples she could relate to. "No questions, let's do it."

Pops smiled, took the triangle and filled in the very bottom line: *Emphasize Evidence*. "The fact is, the fifth rule is crucial to your ultimate success at selling value."

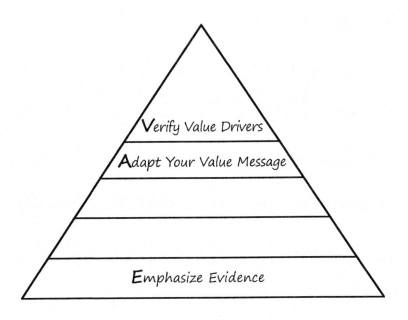

"Why?"

"Because when you provide evidence of value you're answering three questions every buyer expects you to answer." He turned to the second page of the *Book of Reminders* and showed it to Mary.

Answer three questions for the customer: How do I benefit? Why should I care? Compared to what?

"Would you like an example to illustrate this?" asked Pops.

"Of course."

"All right, well, in my second job out of college I sold material supplies to the automotive market. I tried multiple times over a whole year to sell a high-potential prospect on my products, all unsuccessfully. One day the buyer was very blunt with me and said, *As I've told you before, I'm already satisfied with who*

I'm using. So if you want my business then prove to me how I can benefit more from your product than from what I'm using now. Give me some good reasons why I should care to hear what you have to say anyway. If you can't do that, then stop wasting my time.

"He wanted some good reasons why he should hear me out, but what he was really asking for was proof of my product's benefit to him. I didn't recognize it at the time."

"Why not?" Mary asked.

"Good question," answered Pops. "I guess I naïvely believed that my product's advantages would be as clear to him as they were to me. This is rarely the case. Have you ever heard of 'The Curse of Knowledge?'"

Mary shook her head. "The what?"

"It's called 'The Curse of Knowledge.' It was observed in an experiment where people were assigned to either be a *tapper* or a *listener*. The tappers were asked to tap out on a table the beat of well-known songs, such as 'Happy Birthday' and the listener's job was to guess the tune. Before the listeners guessed, tappers were asked to predict the percentage of listeners who would guess correctly. They predicted fifty percent. However, the actual accuracy was less than three percent."

"That's surprising," Mary remarked.

"Not really," Pops said. "Researchers discovered that when the tappers tapped it was impossible to avoid hearing the tune playing themselves. Yet, the listener heard something more like a strange cryptographic beat tapped out on the table. The tappers were shocked at how difficult it was for the listeners to pick out the tune."

"All right, but I don't see how this applies to selling value."

"That's fair," said Pops, "But I wasn't finished. The point is how our knowledge can work against us. You have years of training and experience with your product, and it provides you with a unique understanding of its value.

"This is where it gets tricky, though. When you communicate your value message to a customer they aren't really privy to all your product knowledge and experience. Initially, they don't relate very well to your perspective.

"You may assume that you've made your value message crystal clear and that you have differentiated it successfully from competitors. Unfortunately, your customer may have difficulty picking out what's actually unique or advantageous in your product," said Pops.

"I get it now," said Mary. "My value is known to me, kind of like a well-known tune playing in my head. But my value could be difficult for the customer to recognize if I don't make it expressly clear, and link it with their value drivers."

"Precisely!" Pops complimented. "The customer wants proof of value and your job is to gather relevant evidence and present the positive difference your value can make for them.

"Let's return to my previous story for a moment. Imagine you are my customer and I fail to convince you of my product's value. What's the safest course of action for you to take?"

"That's obvious. Stay with a trusted, current supplier."

"Totally correct," said Pops.

"Then why didn't you Emphasize Evidence and use the proof your company provided to you?" asked Mary.

"Because my employer didn't provide much in the way of proof. And yet, that wasn't a good excuse for *me* not doing it."

Mary shook her head, and said, "I don't agree. Your company should have provided the evidence to you. I'm not provided with the kind of information I need for emphasizing evidence. So how can I sell value if I don't have the supportive evidence I need?"

"Develop it yourself. Take the initiative."

Mary frowned.

"You've heard the expression, 'The proof's in the numbers'?" asked Pops. "It has never been more true than—"

"But—"

"Let me finish, please. The need for sufficient proof of value has never been truer than it is today. Just look at buyers today, and look at society. There's more distrust, more skepticism than ever. Let's go to the Reminder on top of page seven for a minute."

Mary quickly found the Reminder and read it to herself.

Don't sell me your product's differences. Sell me the difference your product makes.

"I remember this," Mary said. "Customers don't care about my product's differences, or its features. They care about the *difference* my product can make for *them*. But where do I get the information to substantiate the difference my product makes?"

"You're out in the marketplace every day. You know the questions customers ask, and you know the objections or skepticisms you deal with. Gather the information that will help you handle objections and customer reluctance," Pops said.

"Okay," Mary sighed, "but can you give me some places to start?"

"Ah, now you're headed in the right direction. For starters, go to your existing customers. Ask them how your product has helped save time, reduced expense and improved their productivity, or whatever else appeals to customers and proves your value.

"Plus," Pops said, "if your company has a lab or R&D department, or a marketing department, ask them for information you can use. Now, can you think of the information or numbers your customers would find helpful?"

"Sure," Mary said. "Numbers on cutting purchase costs, improving inventory turns, and numbers regarding how we help increase sales or profits, improve safety. . ."

Pops smiled and said, "Perfect! Just make certain you present evidence that's truly representative of your company and product capabilities."

"Of course, I see that. But what about intangible benefits like peace of mind, trust, confidence? Use those, too?" Mary asked.

"Absolutely. Intangible advantages increase customer perceived value and can be powerful motivations when it comes to choosing between suppliers. Also offer your customer testimonials and case studies. Provide videos, articles, introduce them to technical support staff – whatever helps, use it."

"You make it sound so easy."

"Maybe you're making it too hard," Pops answered, chuckling. "Let me give you a couple of examples. First, I'll give you a good example to illustrate how easy it is to Emphasize Evidence correctly. Then, we will look at an example of how *not* to do it.

"When we owned the radio station our copier eventually had to be replaced. I called three copier companies. The sales rep who won our business was fantastic. He verified our value drivers with good questions, which gave him a thorough understanding of our situation. Then he offered recommendations and supported it with evidence."

"What kind of evidence did he give you?" asked Mary.

"Customer testimonials, case studies and a comparison chart of cost-per-copy and lifetime wear numbers. He realized that his copiers were more expensive than we had perhaps budgeted," Pops said. "So he provided evidence to quantify the long-term better cost, and the greater value we would receive buying his copier."

"The copier reps who lost the sale failed when it came to Verify Value Drivers, Adapt Your Value Message and Emphasize Evidence, right?" Mary asked.

"Precisely," Pops said with a definite nod. "And you know, his value stood out far above theirs because he could link his value message directly to our value drivers in a convincing way.

"Now, let me give you the example of how *not* to Emphasize Evidence. A few months ago I was shopping for a new camera at a big box store and dealt with a salesperson who considered himself a product expert. And he did seem to know everything about cameras, but it was hard to feel comfortable buying the camera because he overwhelmed me with too much information. Only a small amount of the information was relevant to me."

"Incredible!" Mary said.

Ping!

Mary's cell phone alerted her to a new email. "Sorry, I need to read this," Mary said, turning away from Pops.

She read her email quickly and said, "Great! The decision-maker at Sphere Resources has just agreed to meet with me in a couple of days."

"Tremendous, Mary!"

"Thanks, but we haven't covered everything I'd like to learn. And you didn't get to finish the how-not-to example . . ."

"True, we haven't covered everything and it's hard to learn it all in such a short time. We can discuss this again, whenever.

"Right now, I've got some good news for you," Pops said with excitement. "Tomorrow night I volunteer at the men's shelter, but Chip has agreed to come over and explain the last two rules! I also invited Jeb, but he's taking a client to the Spurs game. Chip will meet you here at six o'clock if that's okay?"

Mary smiled, and said, "You bet." She was pleased that Chip, the younger of her two older brothers, wanted to help.

Mary stood and told Pops goodbye. She gave Chumley one final head scratch before leaving.

Pops watched from the window as Mary drove away.

WHY MEGAVALUE
SELLING WORKS

M ARY SAT ALONE in the bullpen for most of the afternoon. That was what they called the office cubicles for the sales reps at Champs.

She left voicemails for both contact names at AB ProPlastics, and a voicemail for Duncan Quinn at Twig Enterprises.

Mary glanced at her watch and noticed the time, grabbed her briefcase, and left to meet her brother at Pop's house.

Early evening thunderstorms had produced some nasty weather. Mary pulled into Pop's driveway just as Chip bolted from his car in a dead run to the front porch. Mary grabbed her umbrella and walked to the door, dodging puddles along the way.

Chip stood under the porch light fumbling for the key. He had a surfer-like, tanned face, moustache and toned physique. He was the top sales performer for an oil and gas services company and was quickly climbing the career ladder.

"Good to see you, sis," he said, turning to Mary. "Get in here before you melt!" Chip pushed open the big front door and Mary hurried inside.

"I really appreciate you coming from Houston to help me like this," Mary said.

"No sweat. I was in the area anyway, seeing some customers. So you've been learning about Megavalue Selling?"

"Yep," Mary said as she sank down on the plush leather couch. "I'm learning from Pops just like you and Jeb did."

"What do you think so far?"

Mary started to speak but three rapid taps at the door interrupted her. *Knock, knock, knock.*

She looked to the right just as Jeb opened the front door and said, "Anyone home?"

Jeb was Mary's oldest brother and had spent the last four years as a senior regional market manager for a global IT services company. Recently, he had been promoted to Vice President of Sales.

"Pleasant surprise seeing you here!" said Mary looking at her older brother. Jeb was in his early forties with thick brown hair, graying at the temples rapidly.

"Yeah," said Jeb, "my client canceled because he has a sick kid, so here I am."

"Wonderful!" Mary said, excited about having his help.

Chip smiled and said, "Have a seat, Jeb."

Mary grinned as Chumley sauntered into the room. He scurried right past Jeb, pausing a moment to hiss at him before hurrying out.

"I'm not a cat guy," Jeb admitted as Mary and Chip laughed. Everyone knew it, particularly Chumley.

"I was just asking Mary what she thought so far about Megavalue Selling," Chip said.

"It makes a lot of sense," Mary told Jeb. "It has certainly worked for Pops, and for both of you! True?"

"Absolutely," Jeb replied. "It's made a huge difference for me and I give Pops much of the credit."

"Second that!" said Chip. "Isn't Pops amazing when it comes to differentiating and selling the value of, well, nearly anything?"

"No doubt." Jeb looked at Mary. "Has Pops stepped you through the Sales Call Game Plan, yet?"

Mary shook her head. "What's the Sales Call Game Plan?"

"Here, I grabbed one from the office at the last minute," Jeb said as he went to the coat rack and retrieved it.

Mary looked it over as Jeb and Chip explained the Sales Call Game Plan. They showed her how it focused on setting a sales call goal, developing questions to Verify Value Drivers, thinking through the value message and anticipating possible objections, as well as gathering Evidence.

"This is really good," Mary said as she looked it over. "How long does it take to create a game plan?"

"Oh," Chip said as he scratched his chin, "about ten minutes, maybe twenty for some calls."

Jeb nodded. "Changing the subject, but . . ." Jeb said as he looked at Mary, " . . . what did Pops tell you about relating to the customer?"

"I already know about the importance of Verifying Value Drivers," answered Mary.

"Actually I wasn't referring so much to Verify Value Drivers," Jeb said. "I was thinking about Listening."

"Listening?" echoed Mary. "Is that what the L stands for?"

"Yes, it is," Chip smiled. Then he added, "Let me get something Pops would want you to see."

L – LISTEN

WHEN CHIP EMERGED from the back of the house he held a huge pair of plastic, flesh-colored ears. He slipped them over his head and grinned a cheesy grin.

Mary burst out laughing and said, "Where did you get those things?"

"Pops used them in his sales workshops when he taught the *Listen* rule," Chip said, placing them on a nearby sofa table.

As Chip wrote in the next rule, Mary said, "You are kidding right? Pops didn't wear those in his . . ."

Jeb closed his eyes and shook his head, laughing softly.

"For real," Chip said. "Pops used it as a visual to help salespeople remember the four keys to successful listening."

Mary cocked her head and asked, "The four keys? Ears? Sorry, I don't get it . . ."

Chip laughed. "Just hold on a sec, you will. The four keys form an acrostic word - EARS. Each letter represents one of the four keys."

"Okay . . . got it! So what's the E stand for?"

"Engage your customer," Jeb answered. "The best listeners focus the conversation on the customer and her needs, desires, or problems."

"Great listeners don't dominate the conversation – they facilitate it through engaging customers," Chip interjected. "You won't learn about your customer and their values, problems or expectations if you're doing most of the talking."

"Sales meetings should be a two-way conversation not a one-sided pitchy-talk about how great your product is," Mary said.

Jeb smiled. "Exactly. If you like to talk like I do, as most salespeople do, it's not easy to break the habit. Studies show that one of the main factors separating top salespeople from average producers, is listening effectiveness."

"I try to keep two rules on every sales call," Chip added. "Don't talk too much and don't interrupt the customer."

"That's wise," Mary remarked. "What's next, the *A*?"

"The *A*? It stands for *Ask questions*," said Chip. "Here's the thing, it doesn't matter if your conversation is by phone or face-to-face. Asking well-thought out questions in a relaxed way helps ease apprehension, create trust and develop better customer engagement."

"Understood," said Mary. "The question I have is what's a good balance of listening versus time spent talking?"

Jeb smiled. "Good question . . . um, I'd say about seventy-five percent engaging and listening and twenty-five percent talking."

"Really?" Mary said, surprised. "Is that enough time to get your value message across effectively?"

"Totally!" Chip leaned forward and said. "Did Pops tell you about the biggest sale he ever made—when he never spoke a word?"

"What? No, he never told me. Are you serious?"

"Yep! He lost his voice and made the largest sale he had ever landed."

Mary's jaw dropped.

"I didn't know that either!" Jeb said sitting at the edge of his chair.

Chip continued. "That's right. Pops was selling seat coverings to major automobile manufacturers. Two days before he was scheduled to meet with one of the big three American car companies, he lost his voice from laryngitis.

"Here's the thing, since his company couldn't risk cancelling and trying to get his meeting rescheduled, Pops went on to the appointment. For about an hour, whenever the executives asked a question Pops would write out brief answers. He also wrote questions for them to answer. Pops never made a sales pitch because most of his effort went into asking the right questions, listening, and understanding their needs. In the end, he landed a two-million-dollar order."

Jeb shook his head in amazement. "Incredible."

"Awesome story!" Mary said. "It reminds me of one of my favorite Reminders, *Customers must think before they buy and questions make them think.*

"Seems to me, if I ask questions that get buyers truly thinking about their purchase, and about my company's value, and then I link it with their value drivers, I will close more sales."

Jeb smiled, turned toward Chip, and said, "Are you thinking what I'm thinking?"

"You mean . . . who's teaching whom right now?" Chip said smiling.

Jeb nodded. "Sis, you are amazing!"

"Yeah," Chip said, "you're grasping Megavalue Selling much faster than we did!"

"Ha, ha, ha! Nice try!" Mary said. "But I'm not making supper for you two!" she said giggling.

"Now moving on . . . what does the R mean?" Mary took her pen, ready to write, and said with a smile, "Thanks for the Atta girl!"

Chip laughed. "All right, the R stands for *Repeat*. You want to repeat back what the customer says whenever the resulting action on your part is significant, or whenever the information could be misunderstood."

"Any specific instances I might relate with?" Mary said.

"You bet. Here's one you might find very relevant," said Jeb. "Recently a peer of mine lost a big sale because he didn't repeat back important information to his customer. The customer told him to go by their office 'next Friday' and meet the new project manager and discuss the request for proposal. Now let's say today is Tuesday. When is next Friday to you?"

"One week from this coming Friday," answered Mary.

"How about you, Chip?"

"To me, it's this coming Friday, three days from now."

"See the problem?" asked Jeb, looking at Mary.

"Yes. So what happened?"

"Well, my co-worker thought, like you did, that the customer meant ten days later. So when he arrived a week late the customer had already given the job to one of our competitors."

Mary rested her pen on her lap and said, "Maybe I'm making this simpler than it is, but he should have tried saying something like: Would that be Friday the seventh, or the fourteenth?"

Jeb nodded. "Exactly. It's that easy. Okay, let's move on to the S now, unless you have a question . . . "

Mary shook her head.

"Okay, the S stands for *Shut out distractions*," Jeb said.

"Distractions," Mary repeated, making a quick note. "Like phone calls, people, what exactly are you talking about?"

"Well, basically," Jeb said, "there are two types of distractions: environment and mental. Environment distractions include things like incoming phone calls, other conversations going on close by, the customer's personal cell phone going off, email pings, people walking by, and other things happening in an office environment.

"Then there are mental distractions that occur while others are speaking, including daydreaming, or thinking about what you're going to say next as soon as the person stops talking. Another example would be, your cell phone vibrates and you start thinking about who's trying to reach you instead of listening attentively to your customer. Anything to add, Chip?"

"Just one," Chip said. "When we fail to listen effectively, not only do we potentially miss something crucial, but this communicates the wrong message to the customer that—"

"I'm not interested?" Mary interrupted.

Chip smiled, and said, "Yes, and it can tarnish your image."

"Controlling distractions isn't always in our control," Mary said.

"True, many times the distractions are outside of our control," said Jeb. "However, we can control how distractions will affect our attentiveness. Is all this making sense to you?" asked Jeb.

"Absolutely," answered Mary. "There's no doubt the *Listen* rule and *EARS* will help me handle customer conversations better.

"In fact, I'm comfortable with moving on to the next rule, the U," Mary smiled and said. "If it's all right with you."

"Definitely!" Chip said as he grabbed the sheet of paper and began writing in the U on the remaining line. "The U is a doozy," he said with a knowing grin. "A real doozy . . ."

U – UNDERSTAND THE BUY

"**A**LL RIGHT, HERE it is. The U rule is *Understand the Buy*," Chip said.

After he finished, Mary said, "No doubt this works together with the other four rules. But you'll need to explain it to me, and why it's a doozy."

Chip chuckled and said, "No problem! The reason *Understand the Buy* is a doozy is because it brought everything in Megavalue Selling together for me."

"Definitely, me too," Jeb said nodding.

"Why?"

"Because it stresses the three main actions that strongly influence your customer's purchase decision," Chip answered.

"What three actions?" Mary probed.

"First action, identify your customer's decision influencers—the people who have some influence on the decision. Second, identify the specific role each individual will have on the decision."

"Keep something in mind," Jeb interjected. "Once you identify the influencers and have a sense for their impact on the decision, you must then develop a positive relationship with each person and attempt to win them over to your solution. When you do that," Jeb said, "the customer is more inclined to purchase from you because you have cultivated their decision influencers as advocates."

Mary wanted clarification. "Are you saying I should focus on the people who have the final decision-making authority since they determine whether or not I'm awarded the business?"

"Nope, we're not saying that," answered Chip. "Just because a person doesn't have the final authority, doesn't mean they don't still have important influence."

"Chip's right, again," Jeb said. "I'll tell you about an embarrassing mistake I made because it ties in with Chip's point, and it may make this rule more clear for you.

"A few years ago one of my customers asked me to prepare a quote for a project. The company had been happy with our previous work and my relationship with this rep was strong.

U – Understand The Buy

When I asked him how our proposal looked he said, 'You're looking good.' Based on that I felt the sale was mine.

"But what I didn't realize," Jeb said, "was that one of the other decision influencers had recently been given more influence. Instead of being asked to offer suggestions only, as she had on previous software projects, she was given final decision-making authority. Unfortunately, I hadn't invested a sufficient amount of time meeting with her and so she chose a different supplier."

Mary smiled. She admired Jeb's willingness to admit that he wasn't a perfect salesman.

Chip rose from his seat and walked toward the hallway.

"Where are you going?" Mary asked raising her eyebrows.

Chip stopped and said, "Jeb's example reminded me of Pop's list of questions for identifying influencers, and the role each person has in the decision. I'll go get it . . . you may want to use it."

When Chip left the room Mary said to Jeb, "To be honest, I'm a little unclear on the different decision influencer roles. Can you clarify them for me, please?"

"Sure," Jeb said, "happy to help. First of all, there are six main decision influencer roles you want to be familiar with. There are recommenders, end users, committees, coordinators, third parties and power players. You can think of them however you want for your business. This is just how Pops taught them to us. I'll give you a quick recap of each one."

Mary turned a page in her notebook, and said, "Fire away."

Jeb summarized each decision influencer role for Mary:

"*Recommenders* make recommendations about the product or supplier to buy from, and may or may not have decision-making authority. Sort that out with questions and do it consistently.

"*End users* are, as the name suggests, the people in the

company who will use your product or service. Again, you'll find incidences when they have big sway over vendor choice, and situations where they have no effect. An end users' role can quickly change from one project to the next.

"*Committees* can consist of only a few people, or too many! They may or may not represent multiple functions or departments. Determining who has the most influence can be tricky, too. Your best bet may be to meet with each individual and get a better feel for his or her influence."

Jeb noticed the strained look on Mary's face, and said, "You want me to slow down?"

"Nope, this is good stuff. What's next? Coordinators?"

"Works for me," Jeb said.

"*Coordinators* are often in administrative or support roles. They may have little influence on a decision; however, they can help you or hinder you from getting to the right decision influencers. So treat them like VIP's because they can be critical to your success!

"*Third parties* may be brought in for their expertise on big purchases. You could see consultants, engineers or other paid advisors who are utilized to interview and even select suppliers. Word of caution though—sometimes a third party individual wants to exaggerate their actual level of influence. Best to verify their influence with other contacts in the company."

Chip strolled in holding a single sheet of paper and said, "You guys finished?"

"No, we have *Power Players* to cover," Jeb answered. "As the name suggests," he continued, "*Power Players* are the people who can step in and override other people's decisions, at any time. Never assume it's accurate when your contact tells you that his or her boss doesn't have any influence on the decision. When a power player isn't involved, realize they may actually be the driving force behind the decision and assert themselves into the final choice."

"Alright, I have a good grasp of each role," Mary said. "Chip, can you let me see those questions now?"

"Here you go," Chip said as he handed her the single sheet. Mary read the list of sample questions to herself.

- What is your involvement (role) in this decision?

- Who else is involved in this decision and what is their role?

- Who (or whom) makes the final decision?

- Who are the end users, stakeholders in this purchase? What is their role in the decision?

- Is there anyone else who might influence the decision? Your boss, other peers, other departments or leaders?

- Have any new people been included in this decision since we last spoke?

- Are there any upper leaders in your company who have an interest in this decision? Will they possibly have input into the decision at some point?

- If there is a lack of consensus on which supplier to go with, who might then get involved in the final decision?

"How often should I ask these questions?"

"As often as you need to in order to stay informed," answered Jeb.

"Hey," Chip abruptly interrupted. "We never gave you the third action. Remember?"

"Yeah that's right," Mary said. "What is it?"

"The third action is to determine your account's full potential and capitalize on it," Chip answered. "Some studies suggest that less than thirty percent of salespeople acquire their customers' total business, and that leaves the rest to be split among competitors."

Jeb spoke up. "Chip's right. Too many salespeople fall into the trap of *maintaining* an account rather than developing the account into more revenue. This is unfortunate, because there can be a goldmine of business ready to be tapped. Fact is, I've landed millions in added sales by selling to other departments, divisions and locations in my client's operations."

Mary thought about what her brothers were saying. She could think of a number of current customers with more potential than she had captured, and this idea got her excited about the possibilities.

"What do you do when—" Chip started to say. The buzzing of Mary's cell phone interrupted him.

Mary glanced at the number and let it go to voice mail. "Give me a minute guys, please," she said with a frown.

Chip and Jeb watched Mary's facial expression as she listened. Mary shut the phone, and said, "You've got to be kidding me!"

"What's wrong?" Jeb asked.

Mary rolled her eyes. "Oh, my company's co-owner wants to tag along on a sales call with Twig Enterprises—one of my three assigned accounts. I've got enough pressure without . . ."

Mary was in no mood to stick around. As she stood and made her way to the front door, she said, "I need to go, guys. I have to get some sales call planning done for Sphere Resources tomorrow."

Mary hugged and thanked her brothers for helping her.

She turned to leave but Jeb placed his hands on her shoulders and said sympathetically, "Mary, you can do this! We profited greatly from Megavalue Selling, and you will too!"

Chip smiled and looked at her with a reassuring nod.

Jeb wasn't finished. "Remember something. Don't doubt your value. Don't doubt yourself. Doubt your doubts. Use Megavalue Selling and you will prosper."

Mary thanked Jeb and Chip, again. Then she left.

The rain had eased off to a dribble and Mary paid no attention to it as she walked to the car.

Mark Champion's voice mail annoyed her. At the same time, however, she felt more emboldened than ever. She felt ready. Determined.

Jeb's words resonated in her mind.

Doubt your doubts.

Use Megavalue Selling and you will prosper.

PART THREE

APPLYING THE FIVE RULES

TURNED OFF, TUNED OUT

A T NINE O'CLOCK, Henry Barnsdall of QS Supply met with the chemicals purchase team at Sphere Resources. The company wasn't pleased with their present supplier and had called a few chemical suppliers to see what they might offer.

During the meeting, Ed Lennard, Executive Vice President and General Manager, along with his two direct reports, Jim Morris, who headed sales, and Tammy Burton, who managed manufacturing operations, weren't impressed with what they had heard so far. Nothing distinguished QS from the other suppliers except price.

"We're just not ready to make a decision yet," Ed said, standing and extending his hand toward Henry. "We have other suppliers to speak with first."

Henry stood and smiled toward each of the decision influencers. "Thank you for your time. If I need to beat a price please let me know – I'd like a shot at your business," he said.

They thanked Henry and he left.

"I was turned off by Henry's approach," Ed said flatly.

"Me too," Tammy added. "He sounds like most of the sales reps we see. You know the type—early in the conversation they want to brag on their product or lead with their price. I tuned him out."

"I agree with both of you," Jim said. "But do you know when low-price companies like QS potentially become our best choice? It's when other sales reps fail to differentiate their product and prove that their value has meaningful advantages over other companies. At that point, why not just go with QS?"

"You make a good point Jim," Ed said. "So we will cross out QS for now, unless we can't find a supplier that clearly provides better value and then QS may, and I repeat may, be our best choice."

Ed glanced at his watch and said, "Okay, let's meet in thirty minutes. Next up is Champs Chemicals."

SALES CALL: SPHERE RESOURCES

MARY PULLED INTO Sphere Resources twenty minutes early.

Sphere was a large, highly desirable prospect and Mary needed to win their business.

Quickly she reread her Sales Call Game Plan, including the section on her goal for this meeting, the questions to ask, and her possible value message. She also considered any objections that might be raised. She then repeated the five rules of Megavalue Selling to keep them fresh.

As soon as Mary stepped inside the offices of Sphere Resources, an attractive woman in her late twenties with short blonde hair smiled and said pleasantly, "Hi there, can I help you?"

"Yes, I'm Mary Minor with Champs Chemicals and I have an appointment at ten thirty with Mr. Ed Lennard," Mary replied.

In a few minutes the receptionist instructed Mary on how to get to Ed Lennard's office.

DITCH THE PITCH

"Come in," ED Lennard called as soon as he noticed her. He stood and extended his right hand. "I'm Ed Lennard."

"Mary Minor, I'm pleased to meet you, Mr. Lennard."

A frumpy little man in his sixties was how Mary would later picture him in her mind. His distinguished beard was noticeably thicker than the sparse amount of gray hair atop his head. Thin black spectacles made him look more like an introverted accountant than a senior executive of a successful manufacturing business.

After they dispensed with the formalities and agreed to call each other by first names, Ed said, "Have a seat please, Mary."

"Hey, sorry I'm late," a very tall man with a slender build and short dark hair announced as he strolled into the office. "My conference call ran a little long."

"Mary, this is Jim Morris, the Vice President of Marketing and Sales; and Jim, this is Mary with Champs Chemicals," Ed said.

"Nice to meet you, Mary," Jim said as he shook her hand.

After a brief moment of chitchat, Ed Lennard said, "So, let me get straight to the point. What can Champs do for us?"

Mary avoided answering his question until she first understood their value drivers. "First of all, thank you for taking the time to discuss your needs and how we might make a difference for your business. I have a few questions if you don't mind," Mary said.

Ed nodded. "Fire away."

"What interested you in meeting with me today?" asked Mary.

"We are reviewing our supplier relationship and wanted to see what the competition is offering," replied Ed.

"Have you ever considered Champs as a supplier?"

"Not seriously, we haven't," Ed answered honestly.

"Why not?" Mary braced herself.

"That's simple," Ed answered. "We buy the identical products you sell, but from one of your competitors at a cheaper price."

I'll ignore the price issue for now, Mary thought. "When you say you purchase the same products as ours from another supplier, how did you come to the conclusion that they were identical? Did you run comparison performance tests or . . . ?"

Ed seemed surprised. "No, we didn't actually run any tests. What I should have said is, it appeared to me the products were identical because they're supposed to do the same thing."

Jim remained silent. Mary wanted his perspective.

GET THEM TO THINK

"YOU MENTIONED EARLIER that you are reviewing your supplier relationship," Mary said as she looked directly at Jim. "Are there some areas you've been dissatisfied with or possibly unhappy about? Maybe with delivery, product quality, or. . .?"

Jim cleared his throat, and said, "Well, we experienced shipment delays a few times due to the supplier's production issues."

"Production issues," Mary repeated, "as in delivery issues, quality issues or something else?"

"Both actually," Jim said, realizing Mary was not the kind of sales rep to accept dodgy answers. "Three times we received late shipments and product that was not in-spec."

"How did those three late shipments, and out-of-spec product incidents affect your business, your timelines, costs and so forth?"

Ed recognized that Mary's question was a good one, and he admitted, "It was darn expensive. We looked like idiots to our customers. The product being shipped out of spec caught us totally by surprise. To answer your question specifically, supplier delays place pressure on our production costs and overtime expense."

Mary heard the frustration. She pressed her luck. "Have you lost any customers over issues like these?"

"Unfortunately," Jim replied immediately. "Last year we lost a great customer who twice received off-spec material!" he said as he pointed to a large map on the wall. "See those blue shaded areas?" Jim pointed, then looked back at Mary. "That's where our future product expansion is targeted and we can't achieve our sales goals if our brand is compromised by a supplier."

Mary concentrated on the blue areas. "Consequently then, protecting your brand name is critical going forward."

"Absolutely. Maintaining our brand is a top priority," Ed said.

"I agree completely," said Jim. "In the future, our brand can't afford to be tainted by a supplier's issue. This brings me to a question for you," Jim said. "How does your quality compare to other manufacturers' quality?"

"Bottom line," Mary said, "our quality has definite advantages."

Ed frowned at Mary's statement. "Really? Can you actually prove that your quality is better than what we're already getting?"

Before Mary could reply, Jim cut her off.

THE EVIDENCE

"I TOTALLY AGREE WITH Ed," Jim added. "Every sales rep brags on their quality—it's the best, the greatest, the whatever. How do we know your quality is any better than our current supplier?"

"I appreciate your frankness," Mary said calmly. "It's a valid question. Let me share two ways our quality gives you an advantage over other suppliers.

"First, we run each product through two extra tests," Mary said. "This far exceeds the standard practices of other manufacturers and it reduces quality inconsistency considerably. This gives you the confidence that our products will stay within specifications."

Mary stopped and retrieved a one-pager from her briefcase. "Here," she said holding a single sheet of paper, "this simple chart depicts how these additional tests produce more consistent and higher quality products." Mary turned the chart toward Ed.

Ed took the sheet and reviewed it closely. He handed it to Jim with a nod.

As Jim looked the chart over Mary pressed on. "Another advantage to you is that we have the newest, most advanced transfer and container systems in the industry. This virtually eliminates any risk of contaminants infiltrating our products and prevents you from receiving off-spec products."

"Okay, so exactly what's the advantage to us?" Ed asked.

"The advantage?" Mary repeated. "The advantage of our advanced container systems to Sphere is that it prevents contamination to your final product once it's transferred, stored, and then shipped. This reduces your risk of losing customers and revenue."

Jim studied Mary for a long moment, and then he looked away. He liked what he heard.

Ed tapped his pen on the desk several times, apparently thinking about something. "Another concern we have, Mary," Ed looked over his glasses and glanced in Jim's direction, "in using a new supplier is product development. What are you prepared to do to strengthen our product lineup?"

Jim drew in a deep breath and said, "Let me put this in context for you, Mary."

Jim stood and walked over to the sales territory map and examined it as if he was searching for something. "Much of our future success hinges on having an excellent product offering in our traditional markets," Jim said sweeping his hand across the lower half of the United States. "And something else you ought to know," he said with a frown, "is that a couple of our competitors are clobbering our products to death, and it's not just on price. They have a stronger product lineup."

Jim returned to his seat, and said with a serious tone, "My question is can your product line actually benefit our business?"

"Yes, to answer your question. There are two ways we can potentially benefit your business by strengthening your product development effort.

"First of all, our economy line is a valid option for you because it yields solid sales growth for our customers. I can go over the products and results when you're ready. Second, our custom blend program will strengthen your offering and help you retain existing customers as well as land new ones. This may have advantages for your blue-targeted markets, in particular.

"Bottom-line? Our products will enable your salesforce to generate significant sales faster, and help you prevent losing customers to competitors with stronger product offerings," Mary finished.

A soft knock at the door interrupted Mary. "Excuse me," said Ed's assistant, "you wanted to know when the operations meeting had begun."

Ed thanked his assistant and then he turned to Mary, and said, "This has been very informative but I'm afraid we'll need to wrap it up shortly."

Mary realized that she must move quickly or risk losing momentum, entirely. "Are both of you the only decision-makers for chemical purchasing? Or are other people involved?"

"Actually, it's primarily me for now," Ed answered. "Certainly Jim greatly influences my thinking and so does Tammy Burton, our plant manager. Tammy had an unavoidable situation come up and couldn't make it."

"I'd like to meet Tammy if it's possible," Mary said.

"Ed, if Tammy's available now, would you like me to introduce Mary to her since you need to get to your meeting?" Jim offered.

"Great idea," Ed said with a smile. He stood and walked over to Mary and said, "Nice meeting you, Mary. This has been a very helpful meeting. We certainly have some interest in what your company offers. You've given us several things to think about."

"Thank you for taking the time to discuss your needs and how we might possibly serve you. I would certainly be honored to have your business," Mary said with a smile.

The Evidence

As she went with Jim to meet Tammy Burton, Mary's thoughts focused on her main objectives for the moment. *Know each person's role in the decision. Verify their value drivers because they might differ. Win all decision influencers over to my value.*

WIN ALL DECISION INFLUENCERS

Tammy Burton's production area was located in a large building adjacent to the main offices. She told Jim that she'd be happy to meet but only had a few minutes before another meeting.

On the way, Mary wanted to clarify the individual roles in the decision and she wanted a clear understanding of the internal relationships, and who trusted whom. Landing the sale and getting repeat business could be influenced by how well Mary worked with each person—and aligned them with the opportunity.

"Jim correct me if I'm wrong, but it sounds like you and Tammy have significant input into the final decision?"

"Certainly," Jim answered, "but make no mistake, while Ed listens to me, he definitely makes the final call. Tammy and I are on the same page about most decisions. But, what you should also know is that Tammy has more influence around here than she admits," he said with a chuckle. "It's good you're meeting with her because she has Ed's ear on vendors—and he trusts her completely."

Mary made a quick mental note. "When are you planning to make a final decision?"

Jim smiled and said, "Hopefully, in the next thirty days."

Jim made the introductions when he located Tammy out on the production floor. She was a young woman in her late thirties, Mary guessed.

Jim quickly brought Tammy up to speed on their meeting. Then he excused himself to speak with someone nearby.

To identify Tammy's value drivers, Mary asked some of the same questions she had asked Ed and Jim. She also asked about volumes and order timelines. In turn, Tammy asked her about the true capabilities of Champs Chemicals.

"You mentioned delivery performance. What on-time delivery performance can we expect from you guys?" Tammy asked.

"That's a great question," Mary said. "We have one of the best on-time shipping performance records in the industry. Would you like to see a recent performance chart?"

Tammy nodded and said, "Sure."

Mary reached inside her briefcase and withdrew her tablet. In a few seconds she brought the numbers onto the screen, "Our on-time delivery performance is over ninety-seven percent," she said, showing Tammy the data.

"Impressive," said Tammy. "Did you show this to Ed?"

"No, we didn't discuss it." Mary put away her tablet and said. "I'm curious, from your perspective what's most important in a chemical supplier?"

Tammy glanced at her watch and said, "Hmm, that's a good question. In my area, I'm most concerned with product quality and on-time shipments. And one of my biggest concerns . . ." Tammy said, pausing to glance at a forklift going by.

"One of my biggest concerns is responsiveness. When there's

a problem, I want a company that's easy to deal with. Would we deal with you or someone else?"

Mary smiled and said, "I'm your main contact if there are any issues. Plus, I work with a team of great people who'll be coordinating your shipments, reorders, any changes you want . . ."

Tammy glanced at her watch again. Mary could tell that Tammy's mind was elsewhere, and she said, "I realize you only have a few minutes available. I appreciate your taking the time to meet with me on such short notice."

"No problem," Tammy said. "Our vendor decision is very important and we want to make an informed choice. Thank you for reaching out to me."

"It's my pleasure," Mary said. "As a next step, what would you like for me to provide or arrange for you in order to help you make a decision about our products and our potential value to Sphere?"

Tammy smiled warmly. "I'd like to see your plant and meet some of the people I might be dealing with. And I'd like to visit with you in more detail."

Mary seized the opportunity.

ADVANCE THE SALE

MARY WAS EXCITED about the opportunity to meet with Tammy at her plant. "Would one day next week work for you?"

Tammy immediately checked her calendar for an open day and time. Mary confirmed the time on her schedule and said, "Great, I'll meet you at eleven o'clock. Can you stay for lunch, maybe meet some of our team members?"

"Yes, I'd be happy to," Tammy replied.

Tammy thanked Mary for taking the time to discuss the department's needs and then walked her the short distance to Jim.

On the way to the lobby, Jim stopped in the hallway and said to Mary, "You made a positive impression today, and I thought the meeting went very well. We need some time to discuss what you have to offer; and I'd also like to schedule a meeting with you to discuss your product development, economy line, and custom blend offering."

Mary didn't hesitate. She set the first time and date he had available. "Confirmed, I will meet you here one week from today at three o'clock," Mary said as she shook his hand and said goodbye.

CUSTOMER IMPRESSIONS

E<small>D'S OPERATIONS MEETING</small> ended and he made a quick dash to Jim's office. He stepped inside and said, "We had a very productive meeting with Champs Chemicals. Don't you think?"

Jim nodded. "Yes, I agree. I felt very good about the meeting and about their sales rep. In fact, I have a follow-up meeting scheduled next week with her to discuss product development. And Tammy arranged for a plant tour next week," he said.

"Good, good . . . that's very good."

"I'm curious Ed, did you like dealing with Mary?"

"Completely," Ed answered. "I liked how she connected her value with our issues. In the past Champs' sales reps have attempted selling me, but none sold me like she did."

"What do you mean?"

"Her questions were thought provoking, for one thing. Made me really stop and think things through. Not only that, but I liked how she was prepared for whatever objection we threw at her with convincing answers—and it was supported with solid proof."

Jim smiled, agreeing completely with Ed's take.

"Another positive difference," Ed said, "is how she made the discussion about us and our needs rather than about her products. Frankly, I am tired of sales reps whose only concern is to pitch me on their stuff."

"Yeah, me too," Jim said as he rubbed his chin, still thinking about Ed's observations. "Tell you something else I liked. Mary's willingness to raise legitimate issues that we hadn't factored into our decision was insightful for me."

Ed cocked his head, and said, "Like our brand?"

"Exactly, she really got me thinking about how a supplier will impact our brand as we go into our market expansion."

"It impacted me the same way. Anything else?" asked Ed as he turned toward the door.

"Yes, one more thing," Jim replied. "Her value proposition was very clear and it was easy for me to see the potential benefit because she tied each reason back to our concerns. I plan to visit with her in more detail about it when we meet next week."

"Great."

"So what are you going to do?"

"For starters, I want to visit with Tammy and get her thoughts. Then, I'll wait until you and Tammy have your meetings next week—and I may want to tag along on one or both of those meetings myself," Ed said as he walked toward the door.

"As long as their prices are reasonable," Ed continued, "and if everyone is comfortable then, I'll authorize the switch to Champs Chemicals."

"Sounds good," Jim replied.

Two weeks later . . .

There was nothing important for Mary to report to Ethan regarding AB ProPlastics. They had not replied to Mary's email or voicemail messages. Rather than get discouraged, she continued to reach out.

The follow-up meetings with Sphere Resources went great. As a result, Ed Lennard asked Mary for a proposal and promised to have an answer to her within a week.

Soon after, and very much to everyone's surprise, Mary landed an appointment with Duncan Quinn, President of Twig Enterprises.

Ethan passed along the positive news to Mark and Laura. They were stunned by the developments from Mary's efforts.

SALES CALL: TWIG ENTERPRISES

TWIG HAD BEEN a top ten account at one time. In the past, they had purchased bulk chemicals as well as a line of Champs' private label products.

Mary's predecessor, Bob, had lost Twig's business two years ago. The reason, according to Ethan, was his inability to retain an account when a competitor came along offering lower prices.

As Mary pulled into the Twig Enterprises parking lot, she took in a deep breath. In her mind, this sales call would have the biggest impact on her fate at Champs Chemicals.

Mark Champion was unable to accompany Mary as he had intended, and she counted her lucky stars for this, too. Now she could run the meeting the way she wanted to.

As she prepared to exit her car, Mary took one final glance at her Sales Call Game Plan. She reflected briefly on each of the Megavalue Selling rules as she prepared herself for the meeting.

It was time to sell Duncan Quinn.

What was about to transpire, however, had not entered the thoughts of anyone at Champs Chemicals. Not even Mary.

UNDERSTANDING THE CUSTOMER'S SITUATION

MARY SMILED AS she approached the woman sitting at the receptionist's desk. She was older, with gorgeous greying hair.

"May I help you?" the receptionist asked in a friendly, southern accent.

Mary smiled, handed her a business card and said, "I'm here to see Duncan Quinn, please."

The receptionist smiled, dialed his extension, and after a brief discussion said, "Mr. Quinn said for me to send you right up."

Mary found Mr. Quinn's corner office on the top floor, just as the receptionist had explained. She knocked.

"Come in," Duncan Quinn said.

Mary entered the office and found him standing and looking out a large window overlooking a park-like setting below. "You must be Mary," Duncan said, turning around and walking over to shake her hand. "I'm Duncan."

"Mary Minor. It's a pleasure to meet you," Mary responded as she shook his big hand. Duncan had a thick neck, a barrel chest, and big arms. His physique better suited a weight lifter than the pudgy man in his fifties she had visualized.

"I've reserved a small conference room and invited a few

people to join us," Duncan said, smiling briefly as he motioned toward the door. "After you, please."

Duncan led Mary into the conference room and made the introductions around the table. "Mary Minor, this is Brenda Ditch. She oversees our Marketing efforts with retail end-users and our resale program. And this is Alice Grimes. She's our Quality Engineering Manager."

Mary greeted each of the women with a smile and then everyone took a seat. She noticed that Alice, a slightly overweight woman with deep wrinkles and a pinched face, seemed standoffish.

"So what was it you wanted this meeting for, exactly?" Duncan asked, getting straight to the point.

Mary obliged and said, "My objective today is to determine how our product solutions might make a positive difference for Twig. You showed an interest on the phone in how we can increase your inventory turns."

"Yes," Duncan agreed, nodding.

"I'm curious, why is improving inventory turns important to you, and why now?" Mary asked.

Brenda raised her index finger to draw Mary's attention. She was an attractive redhead and Mary estimated they were close in age. "Basically, our inventory levels are high and we need to increase turns, drive top-line growth, and streamline our product offering," Brenda explained.

"That's right," said Alice. "Our most important priority is sales growth, of course, and improving inventory turns is essential. We believe part of the solution also involves consolidating, reformulating, and improving the quality of our product offering so—"

"And let's not forget," Duncan interrupted, "we need to enhance our product rollout efforts in order to counteract what the competition's doing. We have way, way too many lost sales!"

"Please correct me if I'm wrong, but I noted four priorities just now," Mary said glancing at her portfolio. "Drive top-line growth, increase inventory turns, consolidate and improve the quality of Twig's product offering, and rollout new products to counteract competitors who are stealing sales. Is that correct?"

"Yes, those are the four main initiatives," Alice said.

"What's your timeline to accomplish these initiatives?"

"Eighteen months," Alice and Brenda answered in unison. Duncan nodded.

"Eighteen months," Mary repeated, waiting for added comments. When none were offered she said, "So what is your current turn rate?"

Brenda winced. "Uh, we basically . . . essentially maxed out at five-point-eight annual turns. Some product lines are hitting only four turns, while others are in the mid-sevens."

"That's quite a range. So what kind of turn rate would you ideally like to achieve?"

"As high as we can," Duncan snapped.

Brenda frowned, and seemed annoyed by Duncan's answer. "We'd like to hit seven turns in twelve months and then close to eight turns in the following six months," she added.

Mary did some fast mental calculations and said, "If you can see a thirty percent increase on your current turns, you could achieve seven-point-five turns in eighteen months or less, according to my quick calculations."

After a few seconds everyone looked at Mary and agreed.

"What kind of an impact would a thirty percent increase on inventory turns have on achieving your top-line growth initiative?" Mary posed.

Understanding The Customer's Situation

"Obviously very positive," Alice answered as she finished reading a text message on her cell phone.

Duncan leaned in and said, "Mary, you wouldn't be here if our current supplier had helped us improve turn rates. You claimed on our phone call that your customers are seeing thirty percent increases, but can that be substantiated?"

Mary liked Duncan's challenge. She was ready. She leaned forward and opened her briefcase, looked at him, and said, "Yes, I'd be pleased to share these four case studies and several customer testimonials if—"

"No, that's not necessary right now," Duncan said, surprised that she had actually brought some evidence to support her claims. "Leave it with me and I'll read them later."

Brenda glanced at the folder Mary held and said, "I'd like to see those later, too."

Mary started to say something but Duncan raised his hand and stopped her as he stood and walked to the coffee machine in the corner of the room.

INCREASING PERCEIVED VALUE

"So Mary, how long have you been at Champs?" Duncan asked as he selected a flavor of coffee, then pressed the brew button.

"About two years." *Where's he going with this?* she thought.

"That's not very long," Duncan commented, his back still turned. "Would you like a cup of coffee, or a bottle of water?"

"No thank you."

"So how did you get assigned to our account?" asked Duncan.

Mary decided to appeal to their sense of humor rather than answer the question directly. She smiled toward Alice and Brenda. "My boss said he was assigning me to a VIP account and if I failed to land it he was going to fire me!" she said with a soft laugh.

Everyone laughed, including Duncan.

Duncan placed his coffee on a coaster and leaned back in his chair, took a loud sip, and asked, "So how are you going to fix our problem of inventory turns, Mary?"

Brenda walked to the coffee machine and added to Duncan's question, "Personally, I'd like to know more about how your customers have managed to increase turns by thirty percent."

"Great questions," Mary complimented. "Brenda, something you said earlier piqued my curiosity."

"Oh?" Brenda said as she turned to face Mary.

"You mentioned maxing out at five-point-eight turns. Were there any specific reasons why it maxed out there, short of your goals?"

Duncan smiled slightly. He seemed to appreciate Mary's question.

"There were two reasons," Brenda said. "Some of our products have matured in sales and should be replaced. The second reason is due to supplier factors outside of our control." Brenda waited for the final drops of coffee to finish and returned to her seat.

"Supplier reasons?" Mary probed gently.

Brenda placed her cup on a coaster then leaned forward. "Yes, our chemical supplier isn't current with the new certification requirements. Not yet anyway."

Alice chimed in. "No doubt we may be losing sales because of it, but we didn't know where to turn because all chemical suppliers are in the same boat. Aren't they?"

"Yes, all suppliers are required to comply. Fortunately for our customers," Mary said, "as soon as the regulations were introduced we upgraded our product line to satisfy the requirements. Consequently, our customers are now generating considerable sales and new customers."

The three Twig representatives listened closely. Mary realized this was a significant issue for them.

"You've made it clear to me that your initiative to drive top-line growth is crucial," Mary said. "I think, based on what we've discussed so far, it's likely you would quickly generate new revenues and new customers with our compliant products."

"Interesting, very interesting," Duncan said, rubbing his chin. He took a long gulp of coffee, locked his eyes on Mary's and seemed lost in thought. After a few slow nods, he finally said,

"You still haven't told us how your customers are seeing thirty percent increases in their inventory turns with your products."

"I'm happy to do that," Mary said. "There are three ways. First, they sell our certified products, which as I mentioned are generating new sales with existing customers and winning new sales with prospects. Second, our customers are increasing turns by private labeling of our three new products and this—"

"Which products?" Duncan said.

Mary gave everyone a quick overview of the products, especially focusing on how they impacted sales and increased turns.

Alice's eyes widened. She turned toward Brenda and said, "You know, this might be an answer to replacing our LXS line—"

"Yes, I was thinking the exact same thing. We ought to look at our degreasers too – they're getting clobbered," Brenda said.

"Possibly . . . maybe," Duncan added with caution. "Mary, what's the third way?"

Mary smiled and said, "Well the third way our customers are increasing turns is through our economy line. We introduced it two years ago and it has been a significant catalyst for sales."

"How long ago?" Alice asked, distracted now by several new emails on her phone.

"Our economy line was introduced about two years ago," Mary answered patiently.

"But doesn't an economy line scavenge the sales of a premium line?" Brenda asked.

DEALING WITH RESISTANCE

"Not if you position it correctly," Duncan said as he folded his arms across his chest. "I've been saying for a year now that we need to look at an economy line."

Mary agreed and said, "Duncan is correct. An economy line must be positioned effectively. The customers with the greatest success utilize our economy line to phase out sluggish products and outmaneuver low-price competitors. Similar to your initiative to strengthen product offering."

Duncan softened his tone and said, "Okay, so while it may not scavenge the sales of our traditional lines, we will take a margin hit with your economy line. Isn't that right?"

"Actually, no. The margins are excellent for an economy line."

Brenda sat back in her seat. "That's hard to believe."

"I totally understand," Mary said with a smile. She retrieved a binder from her briefcase and flipped through its pages, locating the chart she wanted. "Let me show you a helpful comparison." She turned it around for them to see.

Brenda and Alice leaned forward. Duncan did too.

"This column lists our economy line and its typical markups versus the traditional line and its margins. As you can see," Mary continued, pointing to the evidence, "this leaves you sufficient room to sell profitably, and yet remain competitive in order to win sales."

"Can I take a closer look?" Duncan asked as he motioned for Mary to pass him the binder.

Several moments passed as Duncan examined the chart closely. Then he handed it to Brenda, who looked it over, nodded, and gave Mary a brief smile.

"How are you able to put out an economy line with these kinds of margins?" Duncan asked. "I mean, no insult intended, but are they cheap formulas?"

Mary could feel the hairs bristle on the back of her neck. She remained composed, and answered, "No insult taken. I certainly appreciate your question." She continued, "Not only are the formulas without any compromise, but product performance is terrific."

"And you base that on . . . ?" asked Alice.

"Well, before launching the line we conducted several rounds of in-field tests. We also hired an independent lab to do side-by-side performance comparisons versus competitors. The results were positive so we launched ahead of plan.

"Something else," Mary said as she grabbed her briefcase handle, "you might be interested in the testimonials from customers. I'd be happy to share the lab results and customer testimonials if you want." Mary glanced around the table, waiting for a response.

Duncan played with his coffee cup and said, "We might want to look at those later."

For the next half-hour the group raised several additional questions and concerns with Mary about the company's products and their technical applications. She answered each question and concern thoroughly, and she responded with several questions of her own.

Then Duncan raised the one issue everyone knew would eventually surface.

HANDLING PRICE PUSHBACK

"So what about price, Mary? Your company isn't exactly known as the low-price leader!" Duncan remarked bluntly.

Mary remained unfazed. "Yes, you are correct," she began. "We don't want to be the cheapest supplier around, but we're very competitive and are regarded by many as the best value overall. Our large amount of repeat business is a tribute to companies like Twig who want to deal with a supplier that can make a positive difference for their business."

"That's nice and all, *but*..." Duncan said, pausing to let his words cast a momentary pall on the discussion. "But your pricing is still quite a bit higher than QS Supply." Duncan leaned back in his seat and crossed his arms.

Mary could tell he was hoping that she would cave in to his pressure and meet QS Supply's pricing. Fortunately, she had prepared herself thoroughly for his price pushback and knew exactly how she would handle it.

"Correct. QS Supply offers cheaper pricing. However, based on our discussions today, it's hard for me to imagine your decision would actually be based on the cheapest price," Mary said.

Duncan shook his head, and said, "Obviously we wouldn't

base it on cheapest price alone. But we aren't going to pay premium prices either. We need the best value possible."

"Certainly. And I'm pleased that you insist on the best value," Mary said. "As you pointed out to me, strengthening your product line, increasing inventory turns, growing top-line revenue and stopping lost sales to competitors, are critical for Twig to achieve. I certainly agree, it will require the best value possible from your next chemical supplier."

Duncan eyed Mary directly. He appeared to be concentrating on what she was saying. Duncan finally blinked, and said, "What kind of prices are we talking here?"

Mary was completely prepared for the question. As a gesture of the company's desire to re-earn Twig's trust, Ethan had approved initially giving them the same pricing as the previous contract.

Mary explained the arrangement including the potential cost savings, and then she waited for Duncan's reply.

"I like it," Duncan said after looking at Brenda and Alice and getting favorable nods.

Mary pounced on the opportunity. "Let me recap what we've discussed together. We examined how our economy line, new products, and our certified products will increase your sales, increase Twig's overall turns, prevent lost sales and improve your product offering. I believe the solutions we've identified together will achieve all four of your initiatives, within your timeline.

"I will also personally own each of the solutions we've discussed today; and I am committed to ensure they are implemented on time. If you give me the green light, I can get started immediately."

Silence.

No one said anything for several moments. Mary and Alice kept looking in Duncan's direction.

DECISION TIME

DUNCAN LACED HIS hands behind his head and stared at the ceiling. With surprising suddenness, he said, "Alice how much inventory do we have on hand?"

Alice was caught off-guard. "Well, we have around four weeks of inventory give or take, depending on sales projections," she answered, looking at Brenda for confirmation.

Brenda nodded and said, "Yes, that's about right, Duncan. But I'd need our own branded labels as before . . . "

"Your digital files can be updated immediately," Mary reassured Brenda. "I will make it a priority."

Duncan weighed the pros and cons one last time. Briefly, he considered delaying the decision but realized this would solve nothing.

"Mary, let's get moving on this. I'll send over a purchase order this afternoon," Duncan concluded.

He walked over to Mary with his hand outstretched, wearing a big smile across his face.

Mary smiled back at him. "Thank you for your business. I'm excited to serve Twig and each of you," she said, extending her hand and thanking each person.

"Oh, one more thing Mary," Duncan said. "Who's your boss? Is it Mark Champion, or uh, Ethan, uh—"

"Yes, my sales manager is Ethan Ford. Mark Champion is the President and co-owner," Mary answered.

"Okay, thanks."

"Uh, is there something I can help with?" Mary asked, her heart suddenly racing.

"No, I just want to copy him on the purchase order. What's his email?" asked Duncan. Mary wrote it on the back of her business card.

Duncan smiled and gestured for her to exit the room as he showed her to the lobby and said goodbye.

On the way to her car, Mary's thoughts swirled with nervous excitement.

Did I really just close Twig Enterprises? Is Duncan Quinn actually going to email a purchase order today, or will he back out?

She sat in the car and stared out the windshield for almost a minute. Then she raced back to the office, ecstatic.

CUSTOMER IMPRESSIONS

WALKING IN ON his employees' conversation, Duncan returned to the conference room. "What did you think about our meeting?" he asked.

Brenda smiled instantly and said, "Very good meeting, and I really like Mary. She's very knowledgeable and helpful."

"Totally about the customer," Alice chimed in. "I was very comfortable with her. Felt like I could trust her advice."

"She wasn't like most sales reps," Brenda said. "She came in here wanting to solve our issues versus trying to do a sales job on us."

Duncan smiled. He respected Alice and Brenda immensely and valued their opinions.

"Tell you something I liked," Duncan said. "Mary was ready with solid answers to our concerns. And something else, she came in here with proof for her claims. That kind of effort is important because we don't have the extra time it takes to substantiate their value and quantify the subtle differences among suppliers—"

"Totally agree!" Alice said. "And I also liked her questions. She made me stop and carefully think through our true purchase needs, our decision drivers and our assumptions."

"So both of you were comfortable with switching to Champs?" Duncan asked.

They nodded in unison. "Yes, we were both saying as you walked in that we would have made the same decision," Brenda answered.

Alice added, "Of course we have a long history with Champs Chemicals from before, and that makes it easier. But really, Mary's message synched so convincingly with our four initiatives that it made switching to her a no-brainer for me."

"Good," Duncan complimented. "I had the feeling we were all on the same page, but I was prepared to nix the purchase order if you two had serious reservations."

"Are you going to send over a purchase order today?" Alice asked.

"Yes, right now," Duncan said. He turned and made the short trek to his office, where he got on his personal computer and completed a purchase order.

Mary: Please proceed in setting up our account with the price and terms as agreed. We expect delivery on or about 30 days. Details to follow. Thanks! Duncan Quinn.

He clicked *send* and reached for the phone.

Duncan realized the importance of Twig having good strategic partners. He regretted that he had left things on a sour note with the company's leaders when he abruptly canceled their previous contract. He also hadn't responded to their attempts to reach out ever since.

Duncan placed a call to Ethan Ford. He wanted to make amends.

When the receptionist told him Ethan Ford was not in the office he asked for Mark Champion.

"Just a moment please, Mr. Quinn, I'll see if he's available," the receptionist said.

SPEECHLESS

"MR. CHAMPION, THERE is a Duncan Quinn with Twig Enterprises on line one for you," Mark Champion's receptionist informed him.

Mark pressed the phone to his ear, and said, "Who did you say is calling?"

"A Mr. Duncan Quinn with Twig Enterprises," the receptionist repeated more slowly.

"Okay, yes, tell him I'll be right with him, please."

Champion nervously cleared his throat and grabbed a notepad and pen. *Why is Duncan Quinn calling me? Does this have something to do with Mary? Has she made matters worse?*

"Hello, this is Mark Champion."

"Mark, this is Duncan Quinn at Twig and I'm calling about your sales rep, Mary Minor."

Mark felt a lump form in his throat. "Yes, how can I help you?"

"Well, I'm calling to let you know we met with her today and we are awarding her our chemical business."

"That's outstanding! Thank you. I'm delighted we won your business back," Mark said, shocked by Duncan's announcement.

"Actually, *Mary* won our business back. She was excellent to deal with, and she's a very good representative for your company.

Now, the other reason I'm calling is to reach out and tell you I'd like to have a fresh start on our business relationship. At the time we stopped our purchases I didn't feel like discussing it with you or Mr. Ford. I hope we can put the past behind us."

"Absolutely, consider it in the past," Mark said. "I regret that we disappointed you before, but I want to thank you again for awarding Mary your business."

"You are welcome," Duncan said. "And oh, by the way, you better hold on to her," Duncan said with a chuckle. "Because if it were possible, I'd hire her away from you and have her sell for us!" he added with a big belly laugh.

Mark laughed nervously, and said, "Mary is someone we intend to hold onto, I assure you."

"No doubt!" Duncan said. "Have a good day." *Click.*

Mark sat in stunned silence for several moments. He leaned back in his chair, his mind racing. *How had Mary won Duncan Quinn's business? What exactly had changed about her approach to produce these kinds of results?*

He bolted out the door to Laura's office and told her the news.

After talking about it for several minutes, they made a decision about Mary's fate. Then they called Ethan to run it by him first.

PART FOUR
SUCCESS!
RESULTS

SWEET REDEMPTION

WHEN MARY REACHED the office, the bullpen was busy with activity. She felt uncomfortable when several of her peers stared at her as she walked by.

Her friend John approached her and said, "Hey Mary, Ethan wants to see you!"

Mary nodded and said, "Okay, thanks."

She checked her email first and her eyes went instantly to the e-mail from Duncan Quinn. Her heart pounded until she read, *Purchase Order.* Immediately, she felt relief, and triumph.

Still, Mary couldn't believe that Duncan Quinn had actually sent her a purchase order. She felt like celebrating right there in the bullpen, but thought better of it.

Mary printed off the email from Duncan and walked quickly to Ethan's office.

"Mary! Come on in here," Ethan said. "Congratulations!"

"For what?" Mary said playing coy.

"You know for what. Twig . . . Duncan Quinn!"

"How did you know?"

"After your meeting Duncan called asking for me, and when I wasn't in, he got Mark on the phone."

Mary gasped and took a step back. "You're kidding? What'd he say?"

"Said he was awarding you their business, and he told Mark he thinks you're a great sales rep."

"I can't believe he actually called in here and spoke with Mark," Mary said as she shook her head. "I thought he was just copying you on the purchase order, not calling!" Mary stuck the purchase order out in front of Ethan.

Ethan looked it over. "Fantastic! It's a full truck order." He was still trying to comprehend what Mary had managed to pull off.

"Oh by the way, Mark and Laura want to see you as soon as possible," Ethan said without looking up from the purchase order.

"For what?"

"I can't say. You'll have to speak with them. They're expecting you . . . so go," Ethan said with a huge smile.

Mary stood there for a moment, not moving.

Ethan looked at Mary and motioned for her to leave. "You'll be very pleased. I promise!"

TOTALLY UNEXPECTED

M ARK AND LAURA were in Mark's office looking at a sales territory map.

"Hello," Mary said as she knocked softly on the door.

"Come in, Mary!" Laura said turning to see her.

Mary took a seat across from them and for the next several minutes she listened as they congratulated and bragged on her landing the Twig account. Mark recapped Duncan's call, complimenting her for the way she had represented their company.

Then Mark and Laura took turns apologizing for misjudging her capability. If all that wasn't shocking enough, their decision regarding her future made Mary wonder if she was dreaming.

"Mary," Mark said with a rare smile, "we aren't sure what you did to turn things around, or how you landed Twig so quickly—and who knows maybe you'll also land Sphere Resources, but in any event, we can't lose you. We want you on our salesforce."

"Yes we do," Laura said nodding. "And something else, we are giving you an overdue pay increase, plus a discretionary bonus for winning back the Twig account."

"Thank you very much," Mary said, truly shocked.

"You're welcome Mary, you earned it!" Mark Champion said.

Mary thanked them again and quickly exited before they changed their minds.

OPPORTUNITY

Six months later . . .

IT WAS FRIDAY afternoon at four o'clock and Mary eased into her chair. She reflected on her good fortune as she gazed out the large jutted windows next to her desk.

Although AB ProPlastics had been locked into a contract and wouldn't consider changing suppliers, Mary still closed the Sphere account soon after winning Twig. Mary had also increased sales with several existing accounts and was now on top of the company's sales ladder.

"Hey Mary, got a sec?" Mark Champion asked as he raised his head over the cubicle and smiled.

"Yes sir," Mary said surprised to see him. She stood and walked quickly to catch up to Mark as he walked to his office.

Mary no longer found meetings with Mark or Laura to be stressful. On several occasions they had asked her to join them and Ethan to discuss accounts that the company's reps were struggling with.

However, she could have never foreseen what was about to happen at this meeting. Not in a million years. "Hello Mary, come on in," Laura said enthusiastically.

"We have something we'd like to pass by you," Ethan said

smiling as Mary sat beside him. "We want to offer you a newly created position."

"What position?" Mary asked.

"We'd like you to become a Sales Mentor to the salesforce," Laura announced. "Initially, we want you to work with the least experienced reps on our salesforce."

Mary was flattered.

"You're perfect for the Sales Mentor role," Ethan said. "And our newer reps will learn a lot from you."

Mary was still astonished by the news, and said, "But, but what do you want me to teach them?"

Ethan smiled. "The main thing is to teach them how you sell the value of our products and services. You are incredible at it."

"And show them how to land accounts like Twig and Sphere," Mark added enthusiastically.

"You can also help them increase existing customer business," Ethan said. "A lot of our accounts are long-termers, but as you know, that doesn't mean they are giving us all their business. Teach them how you've increased sales with existing accounts."

"Does it sound like a position you'd like to take on?" Laura asked.

Mary smiled, and said, "Absolutely. When do I start?"

"Let's have you begin immediately," Laura answered. "If it's okay with Ethan . . ."

Ethan stood, and said, "Totally! My thoughts exactly."

SHARING MEGAVALUE SELLING

A FTER WORK MARY drove immediately to Pop's house. She couldn't wait to share the good news in person.

She entered without knocking and hurried to the kitchen where she heard the garbage disposal running. "Hi Pops!" she said enthusiastically. "I've got great news!"

"Mary! I didn't hear you come in!" Pops said as he almost dropped the bowl he was holding.

The news of her promotion delighted Pops. He walked over to give her a hug, and said, "I am so . . . so very proud of you."

"Thanks!" Mary said with a smile that lit up the room.

The father-daughter pair talked for almost two hours. They laughed together at how Mary had initially resisted change, resisted Pop's advice and wanted to quit her job. And, perhaps most important of all, they discussed Mary's new opportunity to help others increase their own success.

Pops beamed. "You have a great opportunity in front of you. Not only will you advance your career with this promotion, but you can also equip others with Megavalue Selling."

"Equip others . . . I like it!" Mary said as she mulled it over.

MOVING ON

In her first full year as the company's Sales Mentor, Mary excelled at helping salespeople increase sales. Eventually, even the seasoned salespeople sought Mary's advice.

She taught everyone who wanted to learn how to use the five rules of Megavalue Selling. As a result, they benefitted considerably.

Mark and Laura Champion noticed Mary's helpfulness, and they were impressed with the results the salesforce had achieved. Sales and profits hit new levels and they gave much of the credit to her.

Eventually, Mary was promoted to Director of Business Development and Training. Once again, she continued to excel at helping others sell the products and services of the company.

She was especially gratified to earn the respect and admiration of her peers, especially in a profession dominated by men.

Ultimately, Ethan took early retirement to move closer to his kids.

Mark and Laura immediately offered Mary the Vice President of Sales role.

Mary declined however in order to launch a sales training

and coaching firm. She turned her energies toward equipping others with the knowledge of Megavalue Selling.

The Champions were disappointed when Mary resigned, but they were also happy for her. They even signed on as her first client.

MANY YEARS LATER . . .

EVENTUALLY, MARY TOOK all the notes she had made regarding Megavalue Selling and turned them into a book. She knew that salespeople didn't have several hours to spend reading a lengthy book. She also realized they appreciated useful ideas they could get results from quickly.

She gave copies to business owners, sales managers, salespeople and entrepreneurs. Mary was happy when they took the knowledge a step further by giving copies to the people in their company, and by doing so, advanced several important goals.

Every salesperson felt prepared. No one felt like they were alone trying to figure out how to adapt successfully to challenges in selling. They were equipped with a roadmap.

They could easily see why Verify Value Drivers, Adapt Your Value Message and Emphasize Evidence worked with customers. And they appreciated being reminded of the essential principles of effective Listening, and Understanding the Buy.

Every salesperson with their own copy could review it as often as they liked, at their own pace and when they had the time. Repetitive learning had paid off tremendously for Mary and it pleased her when others also believed in its importance.

Mary was also thrilled to see salespeople win more sales and land prized accounts. She was happy to see some salespeople incorporate the five rules into their existing sales process, while others used it as the sole concept in a new approach to winning sales.

As Mary drove to Pop's house, she reflected on how fortunate she was to have learned Megavalue Selling from him.

Ring, ring.

Her car phone sounded and she said, "Hello, this is Mary Minor."

"Hello Mary, this is Henry Barnsdall of QS Supply. I'm not sure whether you remember me?"

Mary's mind flashed with memories of losing sales to Henry and QS Supply, her former archrival. "Yes, of course I remember you Henry. I lost a ton of sales to you! How are you doing?"

"Ah, not so well actually. Sales are tough and our profit margins aren't great," Henry said with a noticeable sigh.

"I'm sorry to hear that, Henry. How can I help you?"

"I've been reading your book and uh . . . and I'd like for you to coach me on Megavalue Selling stuff. I may be an old sales dog, but I'm ready to learn some new tricks."

"Henry, I'd be delighted to help you. How about Friday morning?" she heard herself ask.

Soon Mary found herself in Pop's living room and told him about the phone call with Henry Barnsdall of QS Supply.

There was no way in Mary's mind that she could ever repay Pops for all his help and support. But she was determined to do the one thing he had requested . . . *Equip others with Megavalue Selling.*

SUMMARY
The Five Rules

A S CHALLENGING as it is to sell and differentiate value for any product or service, it's not complicated. Keeping it simple is actually very important, whether you sell a technical product, a commodity, or even if you sell professional services like insurance, financial or legal advice. This part of the book is provided so you have a clear, simple guide for using the Five Rules of Megavalue Selling to increase your sales.

V- Verify Value Drivers

Questions should make customers think about the value they truly need.

Accurately identifying the customer's value drivers is the chief priority for a sales professional. Without it, winning the sale is virtually impossible.

Unfortunately, the ability to ask questions effectively is so undervalued, and so under-invested in, that it gets little time in sales meetings, sales training or in sales call preparation. Ironically, studies show that most buyers feel like salespeople bring little or no value to the purchase decision, thus wasting treasured time. Clearly, buyers are frustrated with most of the salespeople they deal with.

Another widespread belief among customers is that all suppliers offer basically the same products and value. This leads to the challenge of how to value differentiate from competitors with similar product offerings at comparable or cheaper prices.

In one significant way, customers haven't changed for over a century: they still want to deal with a salesperson they can trust, someone who will take the time to understand their true needs. The best way to understand the customer's needs, desires, fears and most pressing issues is to Verify Value Drivers.

Tips for Verifying Value Drivers

- Find out who the top decision influencers in each organization are.

- Engage each decision influencer with relevant questions that make them stop and think more thoroughly about the purchase.

- Ask questions that will help build a complete understanding of their needs: What business issues or problems are they facing? What opportunity or goal are they focusing on? What motivated them to meet with you? Why now?

- Review the sample questions in the book and practice them as Mary did. Craft questions that fit your customer.

- Ask the right questions in the right way. To do this, write down several questions you might use. Then review each question. Could it be clearer? Does it have the right tone? Will the question uncover value drivers and issues in the business?

- Keep a journal of questions that work well so you can use them again.

A- Adapt Your Value Message

Customers are won over to a value message for different reasons. Great salespeople adapt their value message to each customer's value drivers. This single talent is so powerful that often you won't need to have product superiority to win a great sales opportunity, but you will need to create high customer perceived value.

At first, Adapting Your Value Message tends to be one of the harder rules of the five to master. And admittedly, it will take time to become proficient with this skill. However, anyone can do it; evidenced by the fact that there are too many success stories from my training and coaching sessions to list them all here.

The following actual example illustrates how profitable this skill can be and how easily it can be used for various opportunities.

For several years I purchased all of my blazers, pants, ties and shirts from one salesman. His name was Rob and he worked in a men's clothing department trying to earn money to pay for college.

I'll never forget the first time I encountered Rob. He had the nerve to say something to me that no other salesman had ever said before. After I tried on a suit, I stood in front of a mirror for several moments. Rob eased over and introduced himself. We spoke briefly and he wanted to know what I thought about the suit. As you might guess, I really wanted to know his honest opinion, and he said, *I think it looks terrible on you.* That's not what you typically hear from a clothing salesperson. Rob could see the surprised look on my face and he immediately began asking questions to understand my value drivers. He asked questions like: *What do you do for a living, Mr. Holmes? How do you want to appear to clients and audiences? What kind of image are you attempting to project? How do you like a suit to feel when you wear it? How long do you want it to last?*

Within the first three minutes he achieved three crucial advantages. He created trust because he was honest, and this gave me the feeling that he wasn't trying to sell me something. Second, he focused on understanding my needs and desires before showing me other suits. Third, by discovering what was important to me, he also learned what should be included, but was not yet a part of my purchase decision (unrealized potential drivers).

Rob knew exactly how to adapt his value message in order to sell to my existing drivers, as well as where to introduce new potential value drivers. The most important thing to remember when adapting your value message is that you are custom fitting a value message to the customer, not the other way around.

By creating trust with me early on, and by understanding my value drivers, Rob won my business. Whenever he suggested purchasing additional shirts, dress slacks and ties to go with the suit or blazer I had chosen, I almost always bought every item he suggested. This added optional looks to my wardrobe and it added sales and commissions for him. In the end it was a win-win, just like it should be when you sell value effectively.

Tips for Adapting Your Value Message

- Review the questions you will ask to identify the customer's value drivers.
- Make a list of the value drivers commonly overlooked by most customers.
- Consider how you will introduce any unrealized value drivers into the discussion and why they are important to the purchase.
- Always link your value to specific issues and drivers. Buyers typically communicate these as negatives and positives (concerns, problems and fears; desires, opportunities and interests).
- Consider how you will deal with possible objections to your value message.

L- Listen

Listening is a choice and a skill that makes selling value easier.

A number of studies find that listening is one of the main factors separating top performing salespeople from average. Most of the salespeople I've accompanied on joint sales calls are experienced, successful salespeople with only average or weak listening skills. This is a detriment to selling value because intentional, effective listening is required.

Several years ago, I interviewed Dr. Lyman Steil, founder of the International Listening Institute. He believed that people can't call on better listening skills just because they want to. Only to the extent that they develop and put listening skills into practice can they be drawn upon for client conversations.

Dr. Steil found that one of the main causes of weak

listening skills among salespeople is the tendency to over-rely on customers to make themselves understood. However, for more effective listening, the sales representative should take ownership of the meeting and be more than fifty percent responsible for the outcome. Simply stated, it's not the buyer's responsibility to convey information clearly enough so that the salesperson has a thorough understanding, but rather the responsibility lies mainly with the seller.

The benefits from effective listening for salespeople include the ability to develop trusting relationships, improve likeability, make a positive impression, process information more accurately, remember facts more clearly, earn respect and create confidence for the solutions offered. To a great extent, this strengthens the salesperson's influence because good listeners don't usually make mistakes like misinterpretation, interrupting people, inattention or daydreaming, all of which can hurt the buyer-seller relationship.

Tips for Listening

- Give your undivided attention. There are plenty of distractions going on in a sales meeting so stay laser-focused on what the customer is saying.

- Repeat back what the buyer tells you, especially when the information is detailed or technical and the risk of misinterpretation is high. By clarifying the meaning of the information with the buyer, you will avoid drawing inaccurate conclusions or forming misguided assumptions about what they have said.

- Take sufficient notes. This will help you review important information and link it to future discussions with the buyer. Better yet, compare it to the information you gather from other decision influencers in the company.

- Take fifty-five percent responsibility for the accuracy of every conversation. Just this extra five percent responsibility will make you more proactive as a listener and will keep you from being distracted or daydreaming.

- Review the simple formula for listening effectiveness found in this book (E.A.R.S.).

U- Understand The Buy

For the salesperson who wants a convincing value message, knowing the customer's buying process is like having the blueprints for constructing a building.

The purchase process for many businesses continues to become more complex. Additional people from more areas of a company now get involved in decisions. Timelines may change suddenly. Purchasing behavior adjusts for changes in the business environment which means less time is available for interacting with salespeople.

A salesperson must be aware of the dynamics affecting a customer's purchase and watch for sudden developments that can create hesitancy, or urgency. It helps to build a thorough understanding of the internal politics, policies and business processes.

Identifying all the potential decision influencers, and then developing positive working relationships with people across the company is also crucial. What's more, a salesperson may need to help people collaborate and reach consensus on the best solution for the company, rather than on what they personally prefer.

Tips for Understanding the Buy

- Know the customer's buying process, their timeline, drivers, issues, politics and supplier loyalties.

- Identify all decision influencers by using the sample questions in this book.

- Develop a positive relationship with each decision influencer. Get an accurate feel for the exact role they will have in the decision.

- Don't automatically assume that individuals who have made decisions in the past are the same ones authorizing the current purchase. *Even experienced reps get burned on this mistake.*

- Work closely with people and try to help them collaborate with one another on the best solution for the company, not just the solution that serves their personal interests.

- Stay informed throughout the entire decision-making process. Don't rely on one person to keep you informed; expand your sources for a complete picture of what's happening.

- Be alert for changes. For example, a leader may claim they have no bearing on the decision but in the final hour they may exert authority over everyone. Change may also occur with the timeline, budgets, or with people leaving (or joining) the process.

E- Emphasize Evidence

Customers put faith in facts not in worn-out claims or everyday sales pitches.

As I was doing the final edits to this book, the national sales manager for a manufacturing client of mine said, "Selling value is good, but how do we differentiate ourselves from competitors who are doing the very same things we are?" This is easier said than done, of course.

No doubt, his question is the most common form of *seller's anxiety* I hear from clients. Still, it's very doubtful that competitors are doing the very same thing, the very same way, with the very same processes, same quality control, same ingredients or formulas. Also doubtful they are using the very same steps, guarantees, storage, delivery, service, field support or providing the very same assurances and peace of mind with the same consistency and value. So, when products are similar, it doesn't mean the value is equal.

There is usually at least one, and most often several points of separation from competitors. Of the many advantages that could be emphasized, a decision influencer is attracted to only a select few that matter to them. Therefore, it's critical to understand the customer's business and be able to focus on key differentiators rather than presenting an avalanche of evidence.

The slight edge at the end of a decision-making process goes to the salesperson who effectively differentiates their value from those of their competitors. Choosing the right evidence for each customer, buying team, department or decision influencer will be a key factor in winning the sale.

It is important to reiterate that buyers will not spend one extra minute of their time quantifying a particular supplier's value. They expect the salesperson to do this.

Tips for Emphasizing Evidence

The book lists several options for collecting evidence. For instance:

- Think about the type of proof your customers would find most helpful and begin collecting this information.

- Gather any customer stories that can help support advantages where no other evidence may exist. For example, it can be tough to come up with convincing data points for customer service, tech support or delivery. But, you can help validate the advantages with good customer testimonials.

- Take sufficient time to run the numbers and do the homework necessary to validate your solution value.

- Customers want convenient options for engagement with content. Format your evidence for use in online, print, digital, or as delivered face-to-face.

- Tone everything for your buyer's individual situation. Do not submit generic materials or evidence unless you are going to explain how it links with their drivers or issues.

MEMORIZE
The 5 Rules

V – Verify Value Drivers

A – Adapt Your Value Message

L – Listen

U – Understand The Buy

E – Emphasize Evidence

ABOUT THE AUTHOR

MARK HOLMES loves helping organizations improve results. With an accomplished record in sales and marketing, he declined the National Sales Manager role with an international energy company and founded Consultant Board in 1986 to pursue his passion for improving sales, sales management, strategic account management, customer experience and leading change. Mark learned business-to-business sales by selling to C-level executives at Fortune 500 companies in his early twenties, became a top producer in three different companies, and held executive positions in sales management, marketing and training.

Mark is on a mission to provide companies with ideas and processes to articulate their value and differentiate themselves from competitors, land strategic accounts and increase sales. The growing appeal of his tools for salespeople and his reputation for sales training keeps him in demand with clients. He specializes in manufacturing, oilfield services, various business services, professional services, insurance, consulting and chemical sales.

He is the author of several books on selling and customer experience including *Wooing Customers Back* and *The Sales Diamond*. Mark has addressed thousands of professionals in twenty industries, and his ideas have been featured in the *Wall*

Street Journal, Sales & Marketing Management, Drake Business Review, FOX Business and many other media outlets.

Mark is a native of southwest Missouri where he lives with his wife and enjoys spending time with their children and grandchildren.

To learn more about Mark visit, www.salesrevenuecoach. com.

MARK HOLMES' SOLUTIONS

BOOKS

The Sales Diamond
Written for any salesperson, this engaging and entertaining quick-read book combines the power of story with four keys to make sales forever.

Wooing Customers Back
This best seller has been utilized by iconic brands like Chick-fil-A, Dunkin' Donuts and Bass Pro to improve service. Written for frontline employees and managers, this simple and compelling story has inspired readers to improve their attitude and actions to give great service.

SERVICES

Training: Hire us to train your salespeople on using effective techniques for differentiating from competitors, selling value, implementing strategic account management or keeping a hopeful attitude.

Consulting: Start an effective change process with us to help your organization improve the sales culture or sales management.

Coaching: Bring us in to coach your salespeople or sales manager. Discuss our special coaching programs for Millennials.

Speaking: Bring Mark Holmes into your company or your convention to speak on articulating value, winning sales and staying motivated.

For more information: www.salesrevenuecoach.com

CPSIA information can be obtained
at www.ICGtesting.com
Printed in the USA
LVOW13s0443250717
542537LV00022B/124/P